THE LITTLE BOOK OF

TRANSFORMATIVE COMMUNITY CONFERENCING

Published titles include:

The Little Book of Restorative Justice: Revised & Updated by
Howard Zehr

The Little Book of Conflict Transformation
by John Paul Lederach

*The Little Book of Family Group Conferences,
New-Zealand Style* by Allan MacRae and Howard Zehr

The Little Book of Strategic Peacebuilding by Lisa Schirch

The Little Book of Strategic Negotiation
by Jayne Seminare Docherty

The Little Book of Circle Processes by Kay Pranis

The Little Book of Contemplative Photography by Howard Zehr

The Little Book of Restorative Discipline for Schools
by Lorraine Stutzman Amstutz and Judy H. Mullet

The Little Book of Trauma Healing by Carolyn Yoder

The Little Book of Biblical Justice by Chris Marshall

The Little Book of Restorative Justice for People in Prison
by Barb Toews

The Little Book of Cool Tools for Hot Topics
by Ron Kraybill and Evelyn Wright

El Pequeño Libro de Justicia Restaurativa by Howard Zehr

The Little Book of Dialogue for Difficult Subjects by Lisa Schirch
and David Campt

The Little Book of Victim Offender Conferencing by Lorraine
Stutzman Amstutz

The Little Book of Restorative Justice for Sexual Abuse
by Judah Oudshoorn with Michelle Jackett
and Lorraine Stutzman Amstutz

*The Big Book of Restorative Justice: Four Classic Justice &
Peacebuilding Books in One Volume* by Howard Zehr, Lorraine
Stutzman Amstutz, Allan MacRae, and Kay Pranis

The Little Books of Justice & Peacebuilding present,
in highly accessible form, key concepts and practices from
the fields of restorative justice, conflict transformation, and
peacebuilding. Written by leaders in these fields, they are
designed for practitioners, students, and anyone interested in
justice, peace, and conflict resolution.

The Little Books of Justice & Peacebuilding series is
a cooperative effort between the Center for Justice and
Peacebuilding of Eastern Mennonite University and publisher
Good Books.

THE LITTLE BOOK OF
TRANSFORMATIVE COMMUNITY CONFERENCING

A Hopeful, Practical Approach to Dialogue

DR. DAVID ANDERSON HOOKER

Good Books

NEW YORK, NEW YORK

Cover photograph by Howard Zehr

Good Books books may be purchased in bulk at special discounts for sales promotion, corporate gifts, fund-raising, or educational purposes. Special editions can also be created to specifications. For details, contact the Special Sales Department, Good Books, 307 West 36th Street, 11th Floor, New York, NY 10018 or info@skyhorsepublishing.com.

Good Books is an imprint of Skyhorse Publishing, Inc.*, a Delaware corporation.

Visit our website at www.goodbooks.com

10 9 8 7 6 5 4 3

Library of Congress Cataloging-in-Publication Data is available on file.

ISBN: 978-1-68099-166-6

e-ISBN: 978-1-68099-167-3

Printed in the United States of America

Table of Contents

Chapter I:
Overview

Greensboro, North Carolina, is a mid-sized city in the southern United States that has been divided by race and class for much of the city's history. At times, the divisions have violently reinforced the separation of different groups. It is also a city with a 100-year tradition of attempts at inclusion and economic advancement—a history that is overshadowed by distant and recent experiences of racialized and class-based violence. The city has been characterized by limited opportunities for effective dialogue on these difficult subjects. Conversely, a counterproductive commitment to civility results in polite conversation about things that matter little, further ostracizing people who want deeper dialogue.

In 2013, a group of Greensboro residents crossed boundaries of race, class, citizenship, and geography to participate in a form of conversation called a *Transformative Community Conference (TCC)*. The results were very encouraging: They created a shared narrative of the community that accounted for the differential impacts that race, ethnicity, class, citizenship, gender, sexuality, and employment have on their day-to-day life experiences. They were able to acknowledge and specifically name the systems and relationship patterns that perpetuated inequities that created violence (i.e., the racial separation that defined the community created a sense of unknowing and insecurity, which resulted in increased police surveillance). They were also able to name the positive, albeit less well known, activities and relationships that pointed toward a more hopeful community (i.e., the occurrence of informal dialogue between some members of the police and undocumented residents that was hosted by a local civil society group). Ultimately, they envisioned a different city based on a broader and more inclusive story. The results of the Transformative Community Conference have become the basis for ongoing efforts to re-shape police/community relationships, explore new approaches to community economic development, and involve local government, businesses, and colleges in welcoming and embracing immigrants and non-citizen residents. The group calls itself the Greensboro Counter Stories Project. While there is much work to do, the TCC approach offers a framework to identify and address difficult issues in hopeful ways.

In **Gainesville, Georgia**, a group of older African American women formed the Newtown Florists' Club to bring attention to the excess death and disease from industrial pollution, which affected both old and young living in their community. Their story was touching and important. They experienced several small and some large victories. Yet, for the first

2

twenty years of the organization, their **problem story**, how people were being abused by local industry and disregarded by local government, was seen as fairly narrow and only of concern to a poor, black, and brown population in one small neighborhood. As a result they had not been able to rally other groups around their agenda. A conversation with several other community groups styled in the framing of a transformative community conference allowed them to spur the development of a multi-racial, cross-class coalition based on broader and more inclusive narratives. TCC helped their cause.

In **Decatur, Georgia**, a small-staffed but nationally focused non-profit organization ("Hometown") was having internal challenges about how to live out their organizational values. The tension divided the staff, creating bitterness and personal animosity. The organization was in danger of losing some of its longest serving and most devoted staff. A strategic planning process that started with a transformative community conferencing framework allowed them to:

a) humanize each other: the people were not the problem;
b) identify the problems: rooted in an incoherent action agenda, and
c) establish trust: needed to make substantial structural changes.

Many communities and organizations that experience divisions are using restorative justice practices to address marginalization based on racial, ethnic, religious, citizenship, and sexual orientation categorizations. Communities often try everything from cross-racial hospitality and dialogue to cultural exploration, system-wide trainings in racialized power analysis, or recognizing implicit biases in an attempt to resolve conflict and violence. In Greensboro, they tried it all, going as far as to implement the first Truth and Reconciliation Commission inside the United States. While each of these efforts makes some contribution to inclusion, equity, and justice, the end seems the same: division, polarization, suspicion, resentment, frustration, and withdrawal. Some wonder: are we condemned to a life of division and inequity? Transformative Community Conferencing is a community engagement and change approach that relies on certain principles that are central to most restorative justice approaches such as inclusive processes and broad consideration of continuing harms. The TCC model extends beyond typical restorative practices by drawing on the power of narrative to connect individual experiences of present harm to systemic and structural sources of harm and to the narrative and societal discourse that gives meaning and sanction to those systems and structures.

What's the Story?

The question of *the story* and *the power of narrative* are being recognized today in transforming conflict and violence as more significant than previously thought. People make meaning of their lives and structure their relationships and aspirations in the form of stories. Events and observations in people's lives are given meaning by placing them inside

4

of currently available stories or by making entirely new stories. The stories we tell most often conform to larger narrative patterns. All narratives have setting, plot, characters, conflicts, and themes. The process of framing all observations and descriptions inside a particular narrative determines what are appropriate behaviors, emotions, and expectations. The Transformative Community Conferencing model takes advantage of the impact of narratives and stories on the life of a community. TCC creates environments where people can come together across previous divides to address difficult issues, imagine, plan for, and work toward a community that has relationships, resource allocation, and create structures that align with their preferred narrative.

> People make meaning of their lives in the form of stories.

Similar to its influence on individuals, narratives guide behavior and emotion in organizations by giving meaning to structures and relationships. In organizations, we relate to others inside the frame of narratives. We pass meaning on to new members of our organization through stories told from within the organizational narrative frame. Most organizations are structured around narratives that become invisible to the people living inside of them. As a result, many structural change processes and efforts to resolve individual episodes of conflict without first understanding the narratives that guide behavior are often ineffective. It may actually be the case that the ways that people know how to live their stories reinforce the very problems they are trying to resolve. The

Transformation happens through the creation of preferred narratives.

Transformative Community Conferencing process invites people to discover previously unconsidered narrative frames that may reinforce or reproduce the problematic conditions and to also identify the presence of events and make observations in different ways that align with their preferred narrative. If people live their lives by narratives, and if organizations and communities are formed through narrative, then it is my belief that they can be *transformed* with the intentional development of narratives that support a preferred experience; they can then determine the relationships, resources, and structures that would support the construction of that preferred reality. Transformative Community Conferencing is a practical approach that contributes to the construction of this preferred reality.

About This Book

This is a Little Book about a big idea. Many communities that have community-wide traumagenic experiences will be structured in ways that have high degrees of systemic inequity. Race, religion, ethnicity, or class often divide people, creating a different quality of life for residents and visitors because of some aspect of their identity. Conflicts often become ingrained in communities, and divisions are maintained by systems whose rationales have long since been abandoned or discredited, and yet, because the divisions are so readily sustained and persistent,

6

hopes for significant change have long since faded. The big idea of this book is this: Even these communities and organizations can be transformed. People, organizations, and communities that have lived with the by-products of societal and cultural trauma, even for several generations, can overcome their history and build equitable communities characterized by respectful and just relationships, inclusive and life-affirming institutions, and sustainable allocations of community resources.

In response to long-standing inequities and communal tension, especially when embedded in systems and structures, **dialogue is almost always necessary but never sufficient to achieve transformation.** People are often given opportunities for dialogue, yet no action results. Participants reflect back that when a dialogue is poorly framed it reinforces divisions, adding to a sense of resignation. Often a community's actions prove inadequate to produce substantial change. Even worse, some action increases negative sense of conflict among people of good will who have different lived experiences, different priorities, and different approaches to transformation. The transformative community conferencing framework presented in this *Little Book* offers communities and organizations hope that there is another future possible.

The *Little Book of Transformative Community Conferencing* offers a practical approach to engaging communities in ways that address conflict and historical, trauma-based divisions.

Transformative Community Conferencing is innovative. In TCC there is acknowledgment of and attention to the need for trust and relationship building. TCC processes identify the power dynamics of structures and stories that shape the experiences of individuals in communities and organizations. It is important to be clear on this point: identifying the difference between TCCs and other processes is not presented to establish one process as superior. It is my contention that each of these processes is important, useful, and valuable; the identification of distinctions is to help the reader select the most appropriate process for the intended work.

Approach	Similar to TCC	Different than TCC
Restorative Justice	(1) Seeks to broadly identify harms. (2) Inclusive processes.	(1) No need to categorize people within victim/ aggressor paradigm. (2) Not focused on accountability for perceived historic injustices, rather, maintains focus on establishing a preferred future and addressing present impediments.

(Chart continued on the next page)

Approach	Similar to TCC	Different than TCC
Narrative Therapy and Narrative Mediation *The Transformative Community Conferencing process draws heavily from the rhythm of narrative therapy[1] and narrative mediation,[2] with a few important distinctions.*	(1) Shares the proposition that the people aren't the problem, the problem is the problem. (2) Uses narrative practices and techniques including: (i) Externalizing conversations. (ii) Double listening. (ii) The construction of preferred narratives.	(1) Focuses on the performative aspect of the collective narratives.
Dialogue Processes	(1) Uses story models that describe lived experiences of participants.	(1) Listens to stories not to establish facts on the ground, but to understand the narrative frame that guide relationships. (2) Focuses on change process and not just increased understanding.
Appreciative Inquiry	(1) Uses current observations as basis for building positive vision of future.	(1) TCCs develop a clear statement of both the problematic narrative and a preferred narrative that supports the positive vision. (2) This also allows for a view of the relations of power that guide and constrain relations.

Beyond simply being an approach to dialogue, TCCs are conducted in ways that naturally provide frameworks for a community action agenda. While a Transformative Community Conference is straight-forward in implementation, it draws on an intricately woven set of theoretical premises, some of which are referenced but not fully developed in this book. The full appreciation of the theoretical principles is not needed to effectively implement a TCC.

Toward Healed and Reconciled Communities

Transformative Community Conferencing is invitational.

Transformative Community Conferencing is a process that is similar in some ways to other healing and reconciling models, community visioning, and peacebuilding or con-flict-resolution approaches. TCCs emphasize the creation of a foundation for further organizational and community healing and reconciliation processes, which might at some point include restorative circles, appreciative inquiry, or any number of other practices. In seeking to establish a sense of wholeness and healthy relationships in a community (i.e., to reconcile), it is important to acknowledge that there are many valuable processes. To determine which to apply, it is helpful to build an overarching framework. TCCs establish the overarching framework, not as exclusion but to support the best application of several other processes.

10

Outline of the Book

Chapter 2: A glossary of terms for TCC: the most effective application of the principles woven into a TCC benefit from the adoption of a few words and metaphors.

Chapter 3: An explanation of qualities specific to TCCs and a discussion of how community narratives function

Chapter 4: An outline of the TCC model

Chapter 5: A description of Part 1 of the TCC model, mapping community and organizational narratives

Chapter 6: A description of Part 2 of the TCC model, creating preferred narratives and action plans

Chapter 7: Skills for TCC facilitators

Chapter 8: Some examples of the application of TCCs

Chapter 9: A conclusion, with some suggestions for how to proceed

Transformative Community Conferencing is an invitational framework for community engagement and analysis. The model is built on three essential distinctions: ***transformation***, ***community***, and ***conference***. In the same way that new narratives can transform relationships and structures, new language can transform our relationship to a circumstance. The next chapter presents the language of a TCC. Each term is vital for the design and implementation of transformative change efforts.

Chapter II:
Word Matters—Glossary
of Terms for LBTCC

Transformation is difficult to establish and unlikely to be sustained when individuals, organizations, and communities continue to operate within the same narrative framework. One way to transform narratives is to change the words and metaphors used to describe or explain a

> **The language of Transformative Community Conferencing**
>
> - Narratives
> - Problem Story
> - Dominant Narratives
> - Preferred Narratives
> - Performative
> - Traumagenic
> - Convener & Facilitator
> - Problematics
> - Reconciliation

context. In this *Little Book,* there are several terms that are intentionally used to shift the reader's view. While the terms might seem awkward at first, the reader is encouraged to use the term, apply the definitions provided below, and not make a mental substitution with a more familiar term. **Let the transformation begin . . .**

Narrative

The term *narrative* is often used interchangeably with the term *story*. The two terms, while very closely linked, are not synonymous. Following Jerome Bruner, TCCs operate from an understanding that "people enact their 'performances of meaning' in their life within the frame of a well-formed story more so than facts or realities."[3] In this way, a narrative refers to the broad outline or general structure of a plot and of certain types of characters. A story is one specific instance within a narrative. For example: the hero's journey is a narrative frame. *The Odyssey, The Wizard of Oz, The Lord of the Rings,* and even the children's stories *Little Red Riding Hood* and *The Little Engine That Could* are each stories told within the arc of the hero's journey narrative. The setting or context, the characters, and the specificity of the conflict will change, but the arc of the narrative remains. When working to transform a community context, a key component is first discovering the narrative structure that is informing current conditions, and then building a broad narrative within which individual community members can direct their individual stories and connect to others.

> Narratives are different than stories.

Problem Story

What makes a story a "problem story"? A ***problem story*** is one where people cannot identify their preferred action because the current narrative does not account for it. If, within the specific narrative frame, the nature of the characters, the direction of the plot, or the framing of the conflict does not offer a perceived sense of agency, the person will experience it as a problem. The characters, context, and plot are representative of culturally defined constructions. The narrative often feels unquestionable.

For instance, in a setting where two heterosexual, married people are choosing to end their relationship, there are culturally defined understandings of the "proper roles" for "husband" and "wife." The problem story is often located in the adherence to those culturally constructed characters. Or more likely, when one party is drawing from one particular narrative (i.e., traditional man) and the other draws from another narrative (i.e., liberated woman), a conflict occurs in the different expectations and range of actions available to each character in the narrative. When trying to transform a context, locating problems inside particular culturally constructed narratives helps us see people as separate from their problems and extends the range of both story formation and actions.

The same event can be storied in many different ways. **It is important to link stories to culturally constructed narratives.** When a problem story can be located outside the person, then preferred narratives can be created, or other stories can be told that support preferred life experiences.

15

Dominant and Preferred Narratives

A narrative or discourse becomes dominant when it is the primary framing through which expectations and explanations about behavior, emotions, and thoughts are determined.

Dominant Narratives: People organize and make sense of their lives inside of narrative frames. Few of those narratives are original constructions. Most of the frames are unconsciously inherited and reinforced by pre-established systems, structures, and relational patterns. An interconnected weaving of multiple narratives is also described as a *discourse*. Narrative theorists identify a discourse as ". . . a system of words, actions, rules, beliefs, and institutions that share common values. Particular discourses sustain particular worldviews. We might even think of a discourse as a worldview in action."[4]

Dominant societal narratives and discourses powerfully influence what gets storied and how it gets storied. Discourses tend to be invisible—taken for granted as part of the fabric of reality.

Transformation is desired when dominant discourses are also problem stories. In communities marked by significant and persistent inequity, it is often the case that the dominant discourse is not a problem story for everyone. It is usually only for those that are advocating for change. The transformation they seek is contained in their preferred narrative.

Preferred Narratives: A person or community's preferred narrative provides a range of choices and actions that:

(a) *validate* equitable relationships, structures, and distribution of resources.
(b) *support* participants in surviving, thriving, and making full contributions within their context.

Community and relational conflicts occur when one person's or one group's preferred narrative is seen as interfering with another's. The object of Transformative Community Conferencing is not necessarily to build a shared preferred narrative for the future in which everyone agrees. Rather, **the intention is to build a broad community narrative that describes a shared future in which multiple preferred narratives can co-exist.**

Performative

The term *performative* is often understood as a variation on the word performance. There is, however, a very important difference related to transformation. The concept of *performative* speech was first described by J. L Austin.[5] A word or expression is said to be *performative* when it actually establishes conditions as opposed to merely reporting on conditions. For example: at the end of a wedding ceremony, when a minister says to a heterosexual couple: "you are now husband and wife," this is not merely reporting on the state of the relationship, it is establishing a condition. Similarly, when a jury declares a person "not guilty," they are not simply reporting on a historical fact, they are establishing the condition of non-guilt. There are many ways that people speak in their circumstances that are less about reporting on conditions than they are about establishing conditions.

Transformation will have performative aspects that are brought out during the Transformative Community Conferencing process. The transformation we put into motion has a quality similar to the Declaration of Independence in the United States. At the time of its writing, the Declaration established a condition that had not previously existed. People subsequently organized their lives and institutions in support of it. In a TCC, when people declare a preferred narrative, it has the potential to have the same impact on relationships, organizations, and communities.

Traumagenic

Traumagenic means to cause trauma. Trauma occurs when circumstances are perceived as life threatening or overwhelming to an individual's or a community's capacity to respond. The circumstance or event itself is not the trauma. Trauma is the complex set of physical, emotional, cognitive, spiritual, and relational responses to an experience of utter helplessness. The distinction between *an event* and *a response* is important because other people can be socialized to mimic the traumatic actions through relational patterns. Also, policies, systems, and structures can be built that pass on and reproduce the trauma patterns of behavior, thought, emotions, and relationships without people or communities directly experiencing the *traumagenic* event or condition.

For instance, if a person almost drowned as a child or watched a close friend drown, this experience might be *traumagenic*. The way trauma would show up behaviorally in their life could be avoidance of pools and beaches. They could also have an emotional rejection of pool parties and beach vacations; they don't like them but do not necessarily connect this to the near death experience as a child. When they become a parent, they might refuse to allow their children to learn

> Trauma is the complex set of physical, emotional, cognitive, spiritual, and relational *responses* to an experience of utter helplessness.

to swim, and the emotional rejection of pools and beaches will be adopted by the children without the children having had the *traumagenic* experience. The trauma behavior, emotions, and thoughts are passed to another generation. In such cases transformation will not include eliminating traumagenic conditions in the second generation; rather, shifting the narratives that structure behavior, thought, and meaning making will be required.

In most instances of community-wide trauma and subsequent inequality, it is not the event that is traumatic, it is the meaning made of the event that makes it traumagenic. If an entire community or group of people experience traumagenic responses, their behaviors, emotions, thought patterns, and even spiritual meanings will be reinforced by others of the group who share similar experiences, or who affirm their reactions. Over time, these behaviors, thoughts, and emotions will come to be described as "normal" and "cultural"; they persist even when the traumagenic conditions have shifted or been totally eliminated.

Convener

The *convener* of a Transformative Community Conference carries out the following tasks:

(a) gathering the background information,
(b) developing the scope of discussion,
(c) beginning to develop a statement of the problematic,
(d) clarifying intentions, and
(e) managing the logistics associated with the gathering.

Conveners may also be facilitators, but not necessarily so.

Facilitator

The *facilitator* is the person or team of people who manage the actual TCC. These would be responsible for managing the flow, timing, energy, and process of shared meaning making that occur during a community conference. In groups and partnerships, there is usually a broad set of diverse assets, which is why it would make sense for someone to be responsible for the convening while others are responsible for facilitating.

Problematic

The term *problematic* is often understood as a fancy academic way of saying *problem*. There is an importance difference. The distinction between problem and problematic is the definiteness of the inquiry. A problem is a question raised for consideration or solution; a problematic describes a circumstance that is difficult to solve because there is no clear formula or pathway for resolution. A problem may be difficult to solve but the answer seems clear; a problematic, on the other hand, is more challenging because it is not even certain that we have named the correct question.

A useful metaphor, used by peacebuilders John Paul and Jill Lederach,[6] might be in the distinction between the solution to a math equation and a chemical solution. While there are specific principles that determine the exact steps that should be taken to find the solution to a math problem, there are many different chemical formulations that can produce certain effects. When a problematic exists, the approach taken is to name the desired effects and then, based on community conditions, determine all of the various combinations of relationships, resources, and

---

A problem **vs.** *a* problematic:

Problem: a question raised for consideration or solution.
Problematic: describes a circumstance that is difficult to solve because there is no clear formula or pathway for resolution.

---

structures that can contribute to the production of the desired effect.

Reconciliation

Reconciliation, problem solving, and healing are the end goals of restorative justice, conflict transformation, and trauma healing, respectively. Understanding where and how to interweave these and other processes to contribute to collective healing and to advance reconciliation is often confusing. The understanding of reconciliation that is embedded in the Transformative Community Conferencing approach helps to clarify how to use the other processes as part of a complex set of actions going forward.

Reconciliation is an interconnected set of processes that have, as shared end goals, the establishment of identities that are:

- relationally constructed;
- authentic;
- dignified;
- interdependently connected;
- legitimated;
- and performatively co-equal.

Relationally constructed means the identities are mutual and reciprocal. *Authentic* identities are self-generated as a result of individual healing and personal or group exploration. *Dignified* describes a circumstance where other people and groups honor the authentic self-expression. *Interdependently connected* emphasizes the ongoing sense of relating,

22

The purpose of Transformative Community Conferencing is building toward healed and reconciled communities and organizations. where relationships are conducted in shared and mutually beneficial spaces. *Legitimated* identities exist in legal, systemic, and structural dignity to the extent that legal, social, and political systems and structures are built and operated in ways that also honor and encourage full self and group expression. Finally, *performatively co-equal*, means that each individual and group has fundamentally full and equal access to the resources needed to survive, thrive, and make a meaningful contribution to society.

Conclusion

Together, these terms—narratives (dominant and preferred), problem story, performative, traumagenic, convener, facilitator, problematics, and reconciliation—provide the language needed for implementing TCCs. Although the terms might be somewhat sophisticated, a certain level of complexity is necessary when dealing with transforming deep-seated inequities in communities. In the next chapter, the question, "What are Transformative Community Conferences?" will be answered.

Chapter III:
What Are Transformative
Community Conferences?

In Transformative Community Conferences, communities, organizations and individuals work together in facilitated discovery to:

a) unveil the major narrative frames that shape their lives;

b) notice the presence of alternative stories that are more in line with their preferred narratives;

c) identify the relationship patterns, modes of resource distribution, and structures that would support the community's preferred narrative; and

d) use their discoveries as the foundation for a community transformation plan.

Qualities of Transformative Community Conferences

The section below describes a few important qualities of TCCs, especially the *transformative* and *community narratives* aspects:

A) *Transformative*

An underlying principle of the Transformative Community Conferencing approach is the hopeful notion that no matter how long certain conditions have existed, with proper focus and commitment, there can be *radical* change. Radical means **at the root**. TCCs plant the seeds and establish the trellis for a new community narrative to flourish.

1. Transformation is not the same as restorative justice.

TCCs reflect the healing emphasis of restorative justice and yet *this is not a restorative approach in the classic sense* of restorative justice. Howard Zehr summarizes restorative justice as "based on an old, commonsense understanding of wrongdoing."[7] Restorative justice is based on a set of principles and practices that focus on victims of wrongdoing, seeking to address the harms they have experienced and creating a space for accountability. The restorative justice paradigm seeks to reorient justice toward the meeting of obligations created by violations. Restorative justice processes are about making things as right as possible. There are several distinctions between TCC and restorative justice.

> Most communities of oppressed and marginalized peoples *do not* want "restoration" but *do* seek "transformation" of their contexts.

The language of restoration, especially in cases of historical and multi-generational trauma and oppression, often gets confusing. Restoration seems to indicate a re-establishment of "better days" when the relationships between different groups were at some point positive, inclusive, respectful, and equitable. Restorative justice is seen as applicable in institutional and community settings where an agreed upon set of rules and standards by which to judge behaviors as wrong or harmful has been established. A primary goal of restorative justice processes is to restore a balance within the context of those agreed upon rules and relational conventions. **However, often the rules that enforced relationships also created the context for harm and are as much a concern as the actual harm.**

In the cases of marginalized populations and deep, long-standing inequities, these rules were usually established by one group and imposed on others.

Also it is usually the dominant narratives, which are perpetuated by rules and conventions that help to sustain inequity. Governing rules and strategies are sometimes based on narratives of inferiority of one group below another. Institutional rules subtlety or blatantly make sense because of dominant narratives that reinforce them.[8] If there was not a mutually agreed upon set of rules and relational covenants, determining who was wrong, accountability becomes more difficult. Transformative Community Conferencing is intentional about involving all sectors of the community in naming and building toward a new community narrative that reflects the equally valued and equitably shared places of all people.

A primary goal of Transformative Community Conferences is to identify or develop preferred narratives that become the basis for the rules and relationships going forward. The operating assumption for TCCs is that communities are co-created and sustained over time by all the actors and institutions. The persistence of oppression and marginalization indicates the need for newly stated shared values, which are not necessarily the values that lead to the need for a TCC process.

French philosopher, Michel Foucault, in his discussion of the relationship between power and knowledge, states: "it is impossible to understand the operation of relations of power of a system from within the system."[9] Or approaching this from another perspective, as people try to study and analyze their own history, it is difficult to do so objectively. How people make sense of life—their reality—is usually shaped by that very reality. The view that we take of what "should be" is constructed based on the history we have received about what is. It is hard, if not impossible, to transform systems and structures if everyone comes from within the same system.

Preferred narratives are also important at the organizational level. In community organizations and institutions, it often appears that a restorative approach is appropriate to restore imbalance, to heal harms. From time to time, however, it is important to update the alignment of organizational values with its relationships, resources, and structures. As the organization or institution is populated by new people, and as contexts change, values and principles that have become hidden need to be revealed. Thus, the ways that values and principles are expressed can be embraced or rejected and updated for the current context.

Transformative Community Conferencing is an engagement model that provides for systems of transformation through an analysis of power and a restated expression of values.

2. Transformation begins at the epicenter.

The intention of Transformative Community Conferences is to radically shift the relations of power of the entire network of systems and institutions that shape current community dynamics. A helpful metaphor for understanding how to begin transformation, first described by John Paul Lederach,[10] is that of an earthquake. An earthquake results from a shift or realignment of the earth's plates. The place where the realignment actually occurs would be described as the *epicenter* of the quake. The impact of the realignment is felt in many different communities and those impacts are the *episodic* effects of the quake.

Communities seeking change often convene around an *episode* of conflict—a police shooting, or a racialized incident, or an act of discrimination, or violence against a child or non-gender conforming adult. Most such incidents reflect multiple sets of problems. To transform an entire community from the vantage point of one event distorts the

> Episodes are symptoms of deeper issues.

nature of the community's narrative. Each episode is a symptom that could be properly identified as one symptomatic representation of the deeper issues. Transformative Community Conferences explore ways to unveil the deeper concerns. When transformation begins from the epicenter, it will have multiple and rippling impacts.

3. Transformation is a long-term process.

Identifying dominant narratives, and establishing or choosing among preferred alternative narratives, can happen in a short time frame, anywhere from a couple of days to a few months. However, transformation takes longer. It occurs when the relationships, resources, and structures are shifted in support of the new, preferred narrative *and* when behaviors,

Narratives point toward transformation, while actions make change.

including thoughts and emotions, have become habitual in favor of the transformed narrative. **The product of TCCs is the explicit stating of a preferred narrative that orients transformative action for a shared future.** It is because transformation is a long-term process that the use of narrative is essential to the success of the work. While the preferred narrative points toward transformation, the daily walk, the actions of community members, makes transformed pathways possible.

B) Community narratives are multidimensional, intersectional, and often "highly visible while still unseen."

Over time, every organization and community takes on a particular "feel." The "feel" is often described as the organizational or community "culture": the ways that people relate to one another, and the presence or centrality of a dominant narrative. There is often even a defining story that serves as the foundational myth or central story of the community. When newcomers and outsiders first experience an organization or visit a community, they become aware of the culture. However, it would be a mistake to assume that awareness of a dominant narrative gives sufficient understanding to prepare for a transformational process. That's because narratives are complex. Community narratives are *multidimensional*,

31

intersectional, and often *"highly visible while still unseen."*

1. Community narratives are multidimensional.

Every community has backstory.

Like a novel, play, or movie, every community has its backstory. There may be larger experiences, often of triumph or tragedy, inclusion or oppression that are central to the community story. But, knowing these central stories won't sufficiently explain the community or organizational culture. The composition of a community changes through birth, death, immigration, and emigration. Organizations evolve through growth, reduction of size, hiring, firing, and changing product and service direction. With these changes there are subtle and sometimes dramatic shifts in the composition of people and identities. However, some unifying stories, values, and institutions remain consistent. What this means is that organizational and community culture is always changing while also sustaining some organizing features.

As people enter a community, they will become aware of visible narratives.

Each individual has a history and a narrative that they contribute to a community. Every person and family is situated differently in relationship to the central events of the community. A static retelling of events doesn't convey the varied impacts, responses to significant events, and everyday organizational arrangements. Changes might benefit some while causing damage to others. What some experience as progress, others experience as a violation of dignity. For example, when a person moves into a community, they might notice the residential patterns and the location of various businesses. The current status can often be explained through a standard retelling of the community's history. However, cultural shifts, like changing housing patterns resulting in demographic variations in local schools, have different impacts on each person, family, department, neighborhood, and ethnic/racial grouping, such as their sense of status, autonomy, relatedness, equity, and even certainty about the future and their place in it.[11] The personal and systematic responses to the changing cultural shift might also reveal some unexamined questions about hidden narratives: what does it mean for people of different racialized, ethnic, or class categories to co-exist in shared residential space?

By allowing for both storytelling and shared narrative construction, Transformative Community Conferencing capitalizes on the multidimensional nature of community narratives.

2. Community narratives are intersectional.

Identity, or the way we see ourselves, is influenced by the stories we tell about ourselves in relationship to dominant and preferred narratives. Personal and group identities are usually formed as a combination of several narratives. A combination of narratives is called a *narrative stream.* In a narrative stream, there are a basic set of stories that influence a person's understanding of their identity, their place and role in an organization or community, which can be based on their age, race, gender, religion, physical

33

Oppression constrains identity, limiting the ways a person can act.

abilities, size, intelligence, family heritage, academic and professional qualifications or certifications, and many other variables. Narrative streams do not usually produce one specific, predetermined identity. However, if most of the narratives in the stream are similar, offering a narrow way of being a man or a woman, young or old, black or white, and so on, it is said to be a *compressed narrative.* [12]

Repression and social inequity result from compressed narratives by reinforcing dominant and oppressive stories. **A compressed narrative is a stream, but a very narrow one, that shapes identities by limiting, for both the actor and those who are observing them, the acceptable or anticipated ways that a person or group can be expected to act, think, and relate.** Compressed narratives are highly resistant to change[13] because oppression is usually invisible, an insidious part of many social institutions. In education arenas, for example, the narrative that a certain class of people is less intelligent will be unconsciously built into the assignment of teachers, the types and amounts of resources provided, and the expectations of the teachers for those students. Even for the students themselves, many of their family members and peers will have accepted the narrative and reinforce it in their interactions, saying things like: "That's not something they let people like us do; you should have realistic expectations for your life; stop trying to be superior."

By way of another example, individual gender roles are learned through interactions with various social systems. There might be a range of roles for girls and women that are taught via narrative stream at home. Those roles may be directly in line with or contradictory to the narrative streams about girls and women at school, or in faith communities, or in the market place.

> The wider the *range* of narrative streams (i.e., the less compressed the narrative stream), the greater the availability of *choice* regarding identity roles.

When identity narratives in a community are more compressed, it is likely that a person will feel more constrained in their behaviors. If a man is told at home, school, and work that women are second-class citizens, he can presumably treat them as such. If a man is raised in a home where men dominate, but finds out at school and the marketplace that gender equity is important, a new and possibly conflicting narrative stream becomes available to him for living out his male identity.

The important point is that each person and each group is comprised of several different intersectional narratives, probably too many to name or number. Some narratives offer more choices than others. The day to day experiences in a community or organization may vary for each person because their identity exists at the intersection of several narrative streams.

35

One characteristic of highly oppressive societies is that there is usually a specific identity feature that overrides consideration of all others. In certain communities because of highly compressed narratives, if a person is perceived to be of a certain ethnic origin, it may not matter how smart, or beautiful, or talented, or innovative they are, their options will be limited. Even two people who share one identity characteristic may experience relationships and institutions in the community very differently. As one example, it is said that "wealth covers a multitude of sins." If a person is wealthy, it often doesn't matter about physical beauty, intelligence, talent, or any number of other factors. And vice verse, in some communities, perceived ethnic or racial heritage will impose limits on the range of expected behaviors regardless of wealth: such as when a professional basketball player who is also perceived as African American or Latino receives extra surveillance in an expensive jewelry store. **Experience occurs at the intersection of several identities, and therefore community narratives that support transformation must be intersectional.**

3. Community narratives are often "highly visible while still unseen."

Conversations disappear. There are certain events and experiences that define an organization or community. Systems will be shifted and relationships are permanently changed in response. While the events may often be discussed near the time they happen, over time the conversations fade. But, the systems hold a permanent record.

In the United States, following what were for some people the traumagenic events of September 11, 2001, someone tried to smuggle liquid explosive onto an airplane, and a similar effort was made to detonate a device that was secreted in the heel of a shoe. Yet, while only being two instances among thousands and thousands of flights, every airport in the United States now restricts the size of liquid containers in carry-on luggage, and every passenger's shoes are screened. Even decades after the initial events, it is very possible that young people and visitors to the country will not know the backstory that shapes these behaviors, but will have to accommodate the results. This is an instance where the conversations disappeared. The performance of the narrative, though, is "highly visible while still unseen."

The narrative practices of Transformative Community Conferences create a conversational rhythm that is slow enough to reveal these narratives, to allow for their systemic exploration. If the relationships and systems served a different time and context, a TCC creates the opportunity to name a new and preferred basis for relationship, a new set of values to undergird the systems and institutions that bind people together in community.

TCC Is *Not the Same* as Dialogue

The shape of the conversation matters. Dialogue can be an important practice in many efforts at community transformation. Dialogue processes provide

37

opportunity to exchange views and get a deeper, richer understanding of the perspective of others. Such dialogue, however, is specifically not designed to advance an action agenda. Dialogue processes can be combined with other more action-oriented processes, but often this feature—privileging relationship over action—frustrates many people who participate. Dialogue processes, often conducted in circles or small groups, are said to have a circular path: There is a problem statement, people express their deepest feelings as it relates to the problem, and then the conversation circles back to the presence of the problem. This is not to diminish the role of dialogue—sharing feelings is an important action step—but the absence of a resulting action agenda often causes people to resist participation.

The purpose of a TCC is to develop a foundation for an action agenda. TCCs have a spiral path. There is relationship and trust building similar to dialogue, but any sharing is done in the service of analysis that in turn establishes a basis for action. A narrative analysis, in the form of a TCC, accomplishes the intention of dialogue by creating opportunity for deep sharing and trust building *and* explicitly moves beyond dialogue, laying the groundwork for future collaborative or coordinated actions.

Like Appreciative Inquiry (see chart in Chapter 1), TCC is a process. The end product of the process is a roadmap or outline for long-term healing and reconciliation at the organizational or community level. Community transformation requires a change in the intention and practice of relationships, a shifting allocation of resources to support new intentions, and a reimagining of structures and systems to align with the preferred narrative. The value of using a TCC is that a narrative-based model creates a natural container for holding and considering multiple dimensions, intersectionalities of identity, and "highly visible while still unseen" conversations.

Conclusion

Transformative Community Conferences:

1. Seek to identify and repair harms by using inclusive processes.
2. Accomplish the primary intentions of dialogue.
3. Reveal the varying impacts that relations of power have within the lived experiences a community.
4. Build shared and preferred narratives.
5. Serve as the foundation for long-term, persistent, and demonstrable transformation.

The next chapter presents an outline of the TCC model.

Chapter IV:
An Outline of the
TCC Model

The shape of Transformative Community Conferencing has benefitted from the earlier works of Gerald Monk and John Winslade (narrative mediation),[14] and David Denborough (narrative therapy).[15] The Transformative Community Conference model is implemented in a spiraling fashion. There is usually more than one round of analysis, which allows the participants an opportunity for deeper reflection. The first round is often conducted as a "practice" dialogue focusing on a play, skit, movie, or some other story-based form (preferably acted out and not just read). The rationale for the practice dialogue is presented further below. The practice dialogue and the "actual" community analysis are conducted following the same steps and rhythm. The primary difference is that during the practice round, there is less depth and no need to build an action plan.

TCCs involve the sharing of stories, which deepen the relationships and experience of participants. Storytelling is introduced in the practice round but is made more personal, specific to the community context, during later rounds of actual analysis.

A Word about Participants

Before describing the steps of the process, it is important to know something about the ideal set of participants for a Transformative Community Conference. To fully understand the scale and impact of the issues that would benefit from a TCC, it is important to get participation from people that experience every level of impact:

- those that are experiencing the harshest and most direct impacts (the marginalized, oppressed, or disenfranchised);
- those who are close enough to the issues to have knowledge and far enough away to have some perspective (often these are advocates, scholars, and allies or sometimes those who were previously experiencing the issues directly but have found themselves in other positions. In organizations this could be a former line worker that is now a manager. In communities this could be a native daughter of one of the disenfranchised communities that has risen in the ranks of power and prestige.);
- those who are at the periphery with limited to no impact;
- and even a few people that would describe themselves as completely unaware of the issues facing their community.

People in the middle group—those who are close enough to the issues to have good awareness and far enough away to have gained perspective—are a "natural constituency" for TCCs. Often these people are local advocates, civic leaders, and academics, already involved in some way with the issues. These are usually the easiest to persuade to be involved. Two groups that are much more difficult to gain both involvement and commitment from but are extremely important to involve in these processes are:

1) those that are directly and most harshly impacted by the inequities; and
2) those that experience no negative impact and may even benefit from the current situation, so have little interest in change.

Ironically, both groups might have the same ultimate assessment about participating: "Not sure how this helps my folks." The first group is often too involved with their day-to-day survival strategies to see any immediate benefit of another "talk session"; the second group has trouble seeing how a solution will be developed without making them "the problem." The fundamental work of the convener is to frame the process in a manner that both groups are willing to try.

Certainly, it is important to have diverse voices and experiences to participate in the same conferencing process. **The greater the variety of perspectives,**

the more fully described and nuanced the community narrative will be. However, if there are too many people to manage at one time, the convener should plan separate conferences, while keeping the widest diversity of voices and experiences present in each convening.

A benefit of convening diverse participation is the creation of an "audience of concern," a group of people who listens to the experiences of the other.

> Transformation begins with hearing each other's stories.

People, especially when they are struggling, want to share their hopes, fears, frustrations, and capabilities through the stories of their lives, hoping that the Others, different from them, hear and affirm their point of view. Affirmation happens even without agreement when someone listens, inquires, and makes connections from the shared story to their own experiences. If the participants are sufficiently diverse it gives the sense that the entire community in some way is affirming the story. Hearing each other's stories: that's the place where transformation begins.

In the next section the basic steps of the model are presented, and after the basic steps, there is a description of two storytelling variations that can also be incorporated, depending on time and level of commitment of the participants. The steps described below would start with a practice round and then be repeated and deepened for the narrative analysis of the participants' actual lived experiences.

Basic Steps of the Model
1. Mapping Community/Organizational Narratives

1.1. Externalizing the conversation: naming the primary problematics
1.2. Mapping the impacts of the problematics in all spheres of life
   • *Story sharing and deep engagement of map**
1.3. Summarizing the impacts of the dominant narrative
1.4. Reverse mapping by identifying unique outcomes as the basis for an alternative story
   • *Unveiling the qualities and context of the unique outcomes that provide the foundation for an alternative narrative*
   • *Story sharing and deep engagement of alternative narratives**
1.5. Comparing dominant and alternative narratives

2. Determining Participants' Preferred Narrative

After conducting several conferences with different participants, the convener can reassemble a representative group from all the conferences to develop a comprehensive community analysis and preferred narrative. The comprehensive version will serve as the basis for design of the community or organizational transformation action plan

3. Building Transformation Strategy*—What is needed to make daily choices in support of the participants' preferred narrative?

- Newly formed or re-imagined relationships?
- Transformed allocation of resources?
- Structural reconsideration or reconfiguration?

These steps are typically conducted in the community analysis and not the practice round. Even though people are alluding to their own experience during the practice round, the story sharing is less confusing if only used in the direct conversations about the community.

Chapters 5 and 6 describe the TCC model in two parts: The first outlines how to map community narratives to identify problematics and dominant and alternative narratives, while the second explains how to select preferred narratives for the purpose of moving forward with transformative action plans.

Chapter V:
The TCC Model–Part 1:
Mapping Narratives

Practice Dialogue

Transformative Community Conferencing usually begins with a 'practice' round. In the practice, the steps of the process are implemented using a "third thing" or "problem posing" material. What Parker Palmer calls a **third thing** or what Paolo Freire describes as **problem-posing material** is something that helps people address their own context by using metaphors from outside their immediate situation. This strengthens their capacity to analyze and transform their circumstances by first allowing them to gain trust and recognize the road they are traveling. Palmer calls it a *third thing* because it is outside of the parties who are in conflict. It is not one party (the first thing) or the other (the second thing), it is a *third* thing. It hopefully creates the space to look objectively and metaphorically, or at least with critical distance, to begin developing insights into one's own context. Educator Parker Palmer often uses a poem, piece of visual or musical art, or sometimes a brief cultural folktale, as a third thing.[16]

Similarly, liberation philosopher and educator Paulo Freire refers to this practice as a *problem posing* method to foster critical thinking. The materials, such as a poster or a skit, often developed by the participants themselves, present the dilemmas or troubling aspects of the problematic without suggesting resolution.[17] Participants are then able to draw insights from a third thing or problem posing for their own context.

For the purposes of the TCC, the starting point, the third thing, is usually a movie or play. The intent of a movie or play is to present a circumstance where there are several challenges and choices, but preferably not a clear resolution. It is possible for the facilitator to arrange for a specific stopping point for the movie or play if it contains a proposed resolution. For instance, not performing the third act of a play or stopping the film after the conflicts and dilemmas have been firmly presented, but well before the solution is offered. Participants will relate to the storyline from different perspectives, often aligning with a particular character, depending on their own personal history and cultural context. To help make sense of unexplained parts of the story participants will create for themselves a *backstory*. One reason to begin with a third thing is to create the opportunity for distance and objectivity that contributes to a clearer view. It might evoke emotions, but those emotions are not directly in response to the person's own lived experiences and day-to-day struggles. An analysis of a movie or play, at the outset of a TCC, demonstrates to participants how *intersectional identities* result in multiple and varied meanings being made from the same set of available observations.

Perspective	Tool for Practice Round	Examples
Parker Palmer	Third Thing	– poem – visual art – folktale
Paolo Friere	Problem-Posing Material	– poster – skit
Transformative Community Conference	Third Thing	– movie – play

The TCC process—conversational structure, process intentions, and mode of community analysis—is usually new to participants. The flow can feel jarring. In the same way it can be jarring for the facilitator. It is recommended that a facilitator practice in advance, to develop experience with the process. In the same way it is good practice for participants to learn the TCC model by applying it to a third thing. Once they witness the power of the model, participants grow more confident in its application and become willing to conduct a deep analysis of their personal context

All of the steps of the actual community analysis are first replicated in the practice dialogue related to the third thing. For better results, participants are encouraged during the practice round to go through the entire conferencing model, other than the story telling and action planning, applying the entire analytical model to the third thing. The mapping does not have to be at the level of depth that it will be for the community analysis. It is very helpful for the participants to see how alternative narratives are teased out of their observations by the facilitator.

1. Mapping Community/Organizational Narratives

1.1 Externalizing Conversations: Naming the Primary Problematics

The process of *externalizing* a problematic is to develop a problem story where the problems are characters in the story and not characteristics of any person or group. One principle of narrative practices including narrative mediation, narrative therapy, and Transformative Community Conferences is that the **facilitators work hard to perceive people as separate from their problems and to help them do the same.**

For instance, as opposed to people being characterized as "fearful of one another," the context could be described as a place where "fear shows up and people react differently" to the presence of fear. In the former description fear is identified as a condition of the people; in the latter instance fear is externalized as a character with its own role to play, actions, and motivations. When fear is its own character, other characters can react differently to it because it is not an essential part of their character. This externalizing process establishes a wider range of options for transforming the context.

Externalizing is done by listening to participants' stories but not by treating the stories as "facts" or symptoms to diagnose; rather, **hearing the ways that stories are told provides clues about how people are currently organizing their lives.** What they find problematic within those stories reveals the places of perceived limitations and hope. The experience of limitation within the story is also a place where the speaker is identifying modes of power that are constraining.

Building an externalizing conversation. The purpose of the externalizing conversation is to have participants name the narratives in which they are living. When participants describe a story while standing outside of it, they become aware of more openings for action than they might perceive while operating from inside the story. Research suggests that being able to see oneself as existing outside the story increases a sense of agency.[18] The effect is one of standing outside the story and peering in it is as though the participant has been offered a new window into which to see their lives. How does one "describe a story while standing outside of it"?

The externalizing conversation begins with a simple declaration:

> The People are not the problem.
> The problem is the problem.

The facilitator begins the conversation with a blank sheet of easel pad paper, writes this assertion at the top of the page, and then draws a large circle in the middle of the page.

51

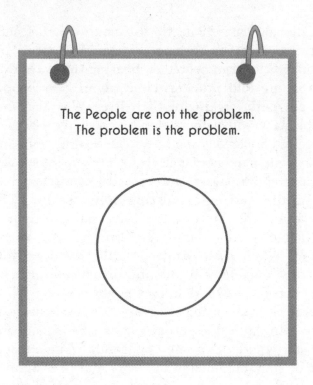

The facilitator then asks a question that invites the participants to consider the circumstance from within this framework:

"If people are NOT the problem and the problem IS the problem, how would you name the problem you saw in the third thing (play or movie)?"

The facilitator listens closely to responses, clarifying and working to make sure that a shared sense of meaning does not suggest that all participants do or should agree with a point that is being made. It

is only to ensure that participants share an understanding of what the speaker intends when they use
certain words and phrases.

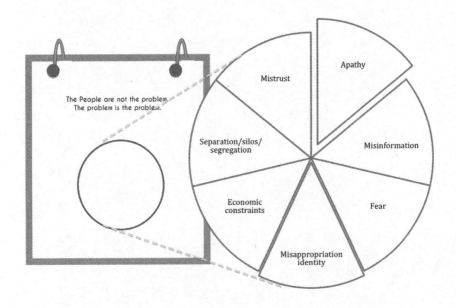

As participants try to identify the problematics,
the facilitator listens to assess whether what is being
named is a description of a *core* problematic or a
symptom, which is better understood as a *result* of a
core problematic. Frequently named core problematics are fear, apathy, resignation, lack of information,
and separation. The convener will write these in the
inner circle. The symptoms, results, and products of
the core problematic will be outside, on "the spokes."
Sometimes an articulated concern could be either a
core problematic description or a result, or both, in the
sense that results also produce secondary symptoms.

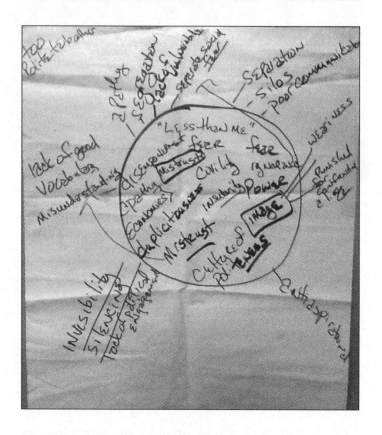

A good example of an issue that a community might identify as both a core problematic and a symptom of the problematic is "separation." Many community members identify conditions where different categories of people (race, ethnicity, class, religion, sometimes even age) live separately. Their day-to-day lives often occur in different parts of the community so that they do not have to interact. Similarly, in organizations separation occurs among people with different functions: legal, marketing, administrative, and so on; organizational separation may also be along racial, gender, or ideological lines. Separation is believed to be the core of many problems because fear, misinformation, structures that privilege one experience or one form of knowledge over others, distrust, and so on, can emerge in response to it. Others would see it as a symptom, emerging from historic narratives of difference, structural arrangements, class pressures, or in the aftermath of government ordinances that enforced separation. In the case of organizations, the nature of a business model might emphasize separation. If one participant names it as a core problematic and another names it as a symptom, the facilitator contributes to the flow of the conversation by pointing out how it could be both. The facilitator will write it in both places, then invite participants back to the task of mapping.

If a problematic can go either on a spoke or in the center, does it really matter where we put the problematic in visual representation of our analysis? One reason to distinguish between core problematics and results is to try to get as close as possible to the *epicenter* of destabilizing conditions. Recall from earlier, an epicenter locates the origin of an earthquake. The closer to the epicenter, the more effective transformation efforts will be.

One way to distinguish between a core problematic and a symptom is to ask participants whether a problematic is a producer or a product. Core issues both negative and positive often have an emotional tag—fear, apathy, love, safety, and trust are clear examples. To help distinguish core problematics from

55

results, a facilitator can ask participants open-ended questions:

- What happens to you in relationships with the Other when "fear" is present?
- What does "fear" invite you to do or not do?
- When "safety" is present, what have you done that you chose not to do compared to when safety was not present?
- When "misinformation" is present, how do people in the organization tend to respond?

The answers to these questions start pointing to the results, symptoms, or products of core problematics. For instance, participants might say:

- *Fear in the presence of my coworkers invites me to be quiet and to avoid those circumstances or even avoid the people* (silence, separation, avoidance, and non communication are symptoms).
- *Fear invites me to protect myself* (products: gated communities, over-policing, increased firearms, hypervigilance, and increased anxiety or defensiveness at work and limited communication).
- *When mistrust is present, I often will not share my ideas; my supervisor then evaluates me as though I don't have ideas. When this happens mistrust usually comes back and brings resentment with her!*

From time to time a facilitator can help participants notice a cyclical pattern:

- **One participant might say:** *"When fear is present, I protect myself; I call the police."*

56

- *The police officer:* "*When I get a call and I think of the potential danger, fear is present; when fear is present I survey the community more and am also more likely to use force.*" (Core: fear; Symptom: increased surveillance and use of force)
- *Another community member:* "*Fear speaks louder when the police are present, and distrust also shows up; both fear and distrust tell me to be quiet or to avoid the police, so I run or keep silent. I also avoid the community members that called the police in the first place, and when I see them, mistrust, anger, and resentment are usually present and talking so loud that its hard for me to hear when they say they care for me.*" (Core: fear; Symptoms: distrust, silence, avoidance, non-cooperation)
- *The police officer:* "*When someone runs, stays silent, or is uncooperative, in addition to fear now distrust also shows up to advise me. Distrust invites me to use even more surveillance and fear tells me to protect myself at all times, which includes increased use of force.*" (Core: fear; Symptoms: increased distrust, increased surveillance and force, and hypervigilance)
- *Back to the first participant:* "*When the police use more surveillance and more force on* those *people, then distrust comes to visit me and tells me I am right to listen to fear, and so I call the police more quickly and more often and I try to keep myself and my family separated from all interactions where fear likes to be present.*" (Core: fear; Symptoms: increased mistrust, increased reliance on government surveillance and force, community isolation, object avoidance, and beginning of a multigenerational strategy of separation).

57

The spiraling nature of the issue points to why it is important to at least try to distinguish between core problematics and results. In the above example, if the community pushes for decreased police surveillance or adopts community-oriented approaches to policing, they are resolving a symptom, but the core aspect of the problematic—fear—is still present. Addressing or changing the climate at the epicenter is necessary, so that *all* community members can better manage their interactions with one another without fear and mistrust.

When developing the narrative of the community problematic it is not necessary to get each distinction exactly correct. Don't quibble over the proper placement, because that might dampen the creative spirit. When action plans are being developed later, certain problematics might be reconsidered in terms of core or symptom. What's most important is to name how problematics are connected to the *relations of power* that are giving life and structure to the community.

A brief word about power

Power reflects the capacity to accomplish a desired outcome. Power is often characterized in one of four ways:

(1) *Power over* is decision-making through hierarchy, force, or repression, often with violence or threat of violence. An economic or emotional sanction might also be the source of how power is wielded.

(2) **Power with** is decision-making through collaborative action. It acknowledges the roles and capacities of alliances. Alliances can be liberating, oppressive ,or simply instrumental.

(3) **Power to** is decision-making resulting from individual and group knowledge, resources, and skills.

(4) **Power within** affirms internal fortitude and resilience as sources of the capacities to achieve.[19]

In the narrative framework of TCCs, **power** is, in the sense that Michel Foucault describes it, "actions acting indirectly on the actions of others."[20] Power is in operation when it causes a person or group to limit actions. If a person or group of people doesn't recognize a certain action as an available choice, they will not pursue that course of action. It is the power of narratives that cause people to conform to narratives without investigating other possibilities.

For example, a female child might be socialized into a community where all of the dominant community narratives present the role of women as performative in the domestic sphere. Systems, laws, relational patterns, and even the religious interpretations reflect this by telling stories of women in the house, raising children, or conducting business only in a market. Even though a girl might enjoy drawing houses and buildings, and imagining new designs for schools where girls could thrive, she might not ask what would be required to become an architect or designer. In this situation, **the power**

of the compressed narrative limits the choices she recognizes as possible. This is *constraining power*. In addition, the socializing institutions in her life—school, faith center, recreational area, and legal system—will reinforce this narrative by the way they make resources available or structure the child's interactions with the outside world. As an adult, she might describe her actions as being her own choice and agency. This would be true in the sense that, within the narratives that she has embraced, *power is acting indirectly* by shaping (in this instance, constraining) her interactions in community. Constraining power guides which institutions she relates to and influences how she conceives of her actions. The female child who likes to draw but is fitted inside a narrative of domestication as the proper role for women will experience her drawing as dreaming of the house she might one day occupy. While a male child in the same circumstance might be encouraged to see this as a house he would one day build, maybe for himself but also for a vocation.

It is important to notice that power does not only act to constrain behavior. The framing of certain narratives will also include productive power. *Productive power* influences people's actions by directing them to act in certain ways whether those actions are serving their best interests or not. Often when telling a story, a participant will say: "I know that my actions didn't help the situation, but what else could I do?" That is an example of productive power. Productive power can also be the source of positive actions in a person or groups' way of being, for example, if a child lives inside of a narrative that includes expectations of performing well in school or being kind and generous. Further, productive power is in action if a narrative does not provide for alternative ways of being, so that a person doesn't even consider acting any other way. As a personal example, I was in the ninth grade before I ever knew it was possible for a child to NOT go to college.

> When participants map problematics, they are simultaneously identifying the effective contours of both *constraining* and *productive* power in dominant community/organizational narratives.

When participants describe results they are pointing to both the limits of and what it takes to overcome constraining power—and how to activate positive productive power embedded in preferred narratives.

1.2 Mapping the Impacts of Problematics in All Spheres of Life

It is important to acknowledge the ways that problematics impact a community. One core problematic can have both affects and effects that impinge on aspects of professional, civic, commercial, and personal life. The mapping stage involves eliciting descriptions of problematics, while visually depicting responses. The figure below presents a schematic representation of the problematic mapping process: placing core issues in the center with spokes to connect core aspects of the problematic to their products, results, and symptoms.

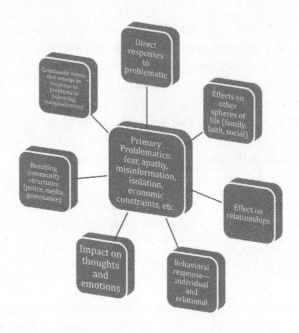

A full mapping may also reflect second- and third-order symptoms:

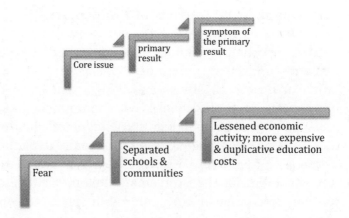

Mapping often reveals how two or more core problematics produce one major symptom:

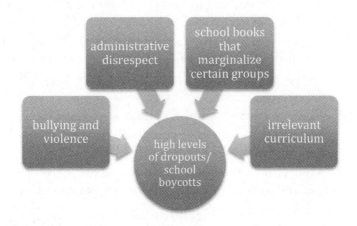

In the example of high levels of dropouts (above), solutions will usually focus on trying to "fix" the children that are dropping out. However, if we start from the TCC mantra that **"people are not the problem, the problem is the problem,"** then creating an inclusive process where diverse voices, especially those directly impacted, get to name the problematics, a different solution will emerge.

In the process of mapping the impacts of problematics, it is easy for specific core issues to get lost. Taking care to consider each core issue and its impacts will provide the participants with a fully textured and well-represented narrative description of their condition. In order to notice the far-ranging impacts of core problematics on a community, the facilitator prompts participants with questions like:

- When fear is present for you, what does it invite you to do or say?
- When there is apathy in the room, how do you act?
- Is it the same or different when you are seeing others responding to the presence of apathy and when you are responding to it yourself?
- What are some examples of how separation impacts *your* thoughts, actions, emotions, or overall life in the community?
- What is an example of how the presence of both fear and lack of information impact your behavior?

The questions above **connect core problems with resulting actions and experiences**. The capacity of the TCC inquiry process to design a transformative strategy will be limited if it does not encourage specific examples. The problematics form a complex interweaving, and therefore, it is likely impossible to highlight a specific outcome solely the product of any one single problematic condition. Even so, it is important to have participants give personal texture to their experiences by seeking to draw the connections.

> Participants are encouraged to use specific examples.

The question framing presented above is **an opportunity for participants to look into both windows and mirrors**, or to look outside their own experiences, as well as to see their own with some distance. The collection of core problematics together with symptoms can soon be described in narrative form (see step 1.3). As a narrative is being developed, it is helpful for the facilitator to share the narrative in its partial form to keep eliciting contributions.

> **Patience is a virtue in the narrative development process.**

The eliciting process should be allowed to go on for some time. As people begin a new way of reflecting on their lived experiences, time will allow contributions to become increasingly insightful. During the mapping process it is important for the facilitator to repeat back the problematics and corresponding results. Slowly, a community narrative will be developed. Each participant might have personally named one or more problematics. They have also affirmed those named by others, by describing the impacts that these other problematics have on their lives. The mapping process is placing each person's story inside the larger community narrative. The personal experiences, nuanced by multiple, intersecting identities, inform the contours of the larger narrative.

1.3. Summarizing the Impacts of the Dominant Narratives

A full, well-textured mapping will include an investigation of the ways that the core problematics impact community and organizational life as well as the quality of participants' lives. Usually, participants are more comfortable describing things that impact their organization or community. Personal impacts are more hidden. Unveiling hidden impacts takes a bit more thought. To help the group make it personal, the facilitator might ask: "In addition to the direct impacts on your life in the community, are there ways in which [fear or apathy or misinformation—name a few of the core problems] impacts your personal relationships?" It is important to give participants some periods for silent reflection on these questions. Examples of questions that unveil hidden impacts include:

- "Are there ways in which the apathy that you feel for the school system changes your relationship with your children or grandchildren in relationship to their education?" For instance, if you have little regard for the schools, what impact does that have on your involvement with homework and extra curricular activities, or participation in school council and parent–teacher conferences?
- "In what circumstances might the presence of a lack of information, or a discomfort in certain settings, impact your social life?"
- "If you have a different understanding of the community than your spouse, or close relatives, how might this affect those relationships?"

Questions can be asked in a large group. It can also happen in smaller groups of two to four people. **In a small group the facilitator might offer a prompt:**

- "Take three minutes each to share a story of a way that one or more of the problematics that we've named has had or is having a *hidden impact* in your life."

Harvesting feelings and insights by sharing hidden impacts can add another layer of nuance and texture to understanding the dominant community narrative.

Example of a textured community narrative:

After mapping the problematics, the facilitator offers back to the group a synthesized narrative. In Greensboro, for instance, after a period of a couple of hours of exploration the facilitator was able to reflect back to the participants the beginning of a community narrative. As the narrative was presented, the facilitator could point to the direct contributions participants made—they could hear their story as part of the larger narrative:

> C = core problematic (written in center)
> S = results, symptoms, outgrowth of problematic (written on spoke)
>
> *Facilitator:* There's fear (c), possibly some ignorance (c), and mistrust (c). There's the duplicitousness (c) around the image of a progressive mystique (s). And if you confront that image, then there's a pushback of the whole power structure (s) that seeks to preserve a particular image (s). And so there's a weariness (s) that comes from that. This mistrust (c), insularity (c), the power, the fear (c) results, and some of the things that it produces, are: separation (s), silos (s), ineffective communication (s), separate social spheres (s), an unwillingness or a lack of tolerance of others (s), a kind of segregation (s), an apathy (s), a whole community

that's "too polite to bother" (s) with some of these concerns. Some of this . . . you know, the fear (c), the mistrust (c), the inability to connect (s) . . . also results in a lack of a good vocabulary (s) for relating to and continuing to process this stuff, so there is continuing misunderstanding (s) that says to some people that you are "less than me (s)." And then there are certain groups for whom silencing (s), a lack of political engagement (s) and even invisibility (s) are the result; and all this creates a kind of an anti-aspirational (s) atmosphere to some extent.

After the facilitator summarizes the dominant narrative, alternative stories are explored.

1.4 Reverse Mapping: Identifying Unique Outcomes as the Basis for an Alternative Story

When people have lived or worked in difficult circumstances for a long time, the difficulty often assumes a central role in how experiences of the context are described. When people talk about a toxic workplace, narratives are often compressed. The storytelling consistently focuses on dysfunction, struggle, and frustration. When people talk about persistent inequalities in a community, narratives are usually compressed toward blame and pain. Narratives, in turn, will influence how people behave in a context.

The power of narratives is that they can either limit or liberate the range of available actions. When narratives shaped by negative conflict dominate a context, unhealthy relationships stabilize in place and seem unchangeable. As new members of the organization or community are brought in, they are recruited to one side or another of a conflict narrative. They are often taught how to act (training/orientation), while the narratives that shape those actions remain invisible. A central activity of the Transformative Community Conference process is to allow participants to uncover different experiences and actions that run counter to the dominant narrative. Alternative narratives offer hope that transformation is possible.

Alternative narratives create hope.

Alternative narratives describe *unique outcomes* and are the basis for transforming a context. While looking for alternative narratives or unique outcomes, Michael White, a social worker and early pioneer of narrative therapy processes, encourages facilitators to select a recent experience.[21] An event that is recent helps the storyteller realize that performing different narratives is possible. Recognizing alternatives in the recent past builds momentum to identify other unique outcomes. Multiple unique outcomes create several points with which to build an alternative narrative. The presence of more unique points, especially diverse and recent ones, allows for the development of one or more well-textured alternative narratives. Also, any set of unique outcomes can be tied together in a variety of ways to populate more than one alternative narrative.

1.5. Comparing Dominant and Alternative Narratives

People live into stories. When their lived experience in a community or organization is dominated by one compressed narrative, they often do not see alternatives for action and lose hope of change. Most systems, structures, and relational patterns exist within the logic of one particular, dominant way of thinking. It is often hard to discover other options for acting. When unique outcomes are lifted up and then placed together in ways that support a narrative that is different from the dominating problem narrative, people can imagine different ways of action. If the alternative narrative is drawn from their own unique experiences of the community (even if uncommon or rare), more transformative ways of being and acting are more accessible and believable. **The construction of alternative narratives becomes the start for considering new ways of action. It is a primary purpose of the TCC method.** Once more than one alternative narrative has been developed, it is essential to have the participants state their preferred narrative.

Conclusion

Through patience and careful facilitation, participants have now shared core problematics, results, and impacts. The facilitator has visually depicted, or mapped, their responses. Participants have described the influences of constraining and productive power. The facilitator has summarized input in the form of a dominant narrative. The facilitator has then invited participants to think about unique outcomes of alternative, more hopeful narratives. The next chapter will move into the TCC stages of determining participants' preferred narrative, in order to build an action plan, or a transformative strategy.

Chapter VI:
The TCC Model–Part 2:
From Mapping to Action Planning

Participants have now identified one or more alternative narratives in contrast with dominant ones. The next step is helping people choose. The selected alternative narrative should clearly indicate new ways of action.

2. Determining Participants' Preferred Narratives

It is important to have participants state their preference from among the available alternative narratives. Participants will often remark that the choice feels "obvious." It is the facilitator's responsibility to remind the participants, that every action they make, in terms of relationships, use of resources, and ways that they interact with or accept current systems, can be understood as expressions of a narrative preference:

"Every time you allow yourself to be silent in response to the presence of fear or misunderstanding or civility or choose to avoid interacting with certain people or places, you are choosing one narrative over the other."

To strengthen the relationship to the preferred narrative, the facilitator should make the alternative narrative more present:

"If this narrative became the dominant narrative for the organization, what would be possible that is not currently possible?"

"What are specific choices you could make if this were the dominant narrative and not that?"

The tendency is for participants to offer glowing, broad, and vague responses, what one colleague calls "glittering fuzzballs", such as: "We would be more trusting," or "We would enjoy being with each other," or "We would be less afraid or less violent." To make the alternative narrative realistic, or at least to make it more compelling, it is important that the facilitator ask for specific actions or outcomes.

"What is one specific thing that you would do if trust was more fully present or present more often?"

"If fear was not as loud in the midst of staff meetings, what are two specific actions that you would be willing to take so that other people would experience you acting without the influence of fear or mistrust?"

Essentially, the facilitator is helping participants map potential impacts of an alternative narrative.

"If she acted that way to demonstrate that she was not listening to fear or hiding behind mistrust, what action would you be willing to commit to in order to encourage a new relational pattern?"

The types of questions that the facilitators ask to make the alternative narrative textured and realistic also help transition the process to building an action plan. The transformation sought in TCCs aims for a culture change, a new way of doing things, *and* a new way of relating. When a new, alternative narrative is collectively and collaboratively developed, consciously chosen, and deliberatively reinforced, talk will become transformative action.

Preferred narratives are the foundation for a transformation strategy.

3. Building a Transformation Strategy

The final phase of the TCC process is the building of an action plan. The action plan should deliberately and strategically reinforce the choices needed for participants to move into the new, preferred, alternative narrative. Simply naming an alternative narrative is important but insufficient to result in transformation. Remember, conversations disappear; as a result actions that align with and reproduce the dominant narratives over time have become a matter of habit. To substitute one set of habits for another will require many reminders and reinforcements.

Culture can be shifted and new habits formed by:

• changing relational patterns;
• reallocating/redistributing resources; and
• reshaping structures.

Action plans should respond to the core problematics driving the dominant narrative and the core values that give rise to the alternative narratives.

"What are the relationship, resources, and structural changes needed to eliminate or mitigate the effects of the core problematics and produce or amplify the effects of the core drivers of the alternatives?"

Narratives are produced and reproduced not just as a matter of speaking and thought, but also through the constraining and productive power of structures and systems. Structures organize interactions between and among people. To develop an effective action plan is a process, likely requiring at least one, if not several, sessions. After the first and second conferencing sessions (Mapping Narratives and Determining Participants' Preferred Narrative), it is sometimes helpful to give participants an opportunity to go back to work, or back to their day-to-day lives, with the explicit task of thinking about variations of the above question, as well as the following:

> **"What are the relationships, resources, and structures that we need to pay attention to in order to decrease the dominant narrative and increase the preferred narrative?"**

> **"Or, what relationships, resources, and structures do we need to transform to make it more likely that people would make choices that act in alignment with the preferred narrative?"**

Through narrative clarity formed during the TCC, and the connections made between certain narratives regarding relationships, resources, and structures, over time it will make more sense which transformative strategies are likely to be most impactful. As participants respond to the above questions, it is likely they will think of other appropriate organizational development, healing, and education strategies needed for change. By collecting participant responses to questions about relational patterns, reallocating or redistributing resources, and reshaping structures, the facilitator builds a transformation strategy.

> It becomes easier to change rigid power structures when an alternative narrative provides a rationale. Thus, appropriate alternative narratives build momentum for concrete action plans.

Summary of a TCC Process

Stage of Process	Key Activities	Central Questions
Convening	- Identify broad spectrum of community or organization voices. - Convene cross border boundary leadership group.	- Who is directly impacted? - Who is at the periphery? - Who is unaware? - Are we ready to seek transformation?
Externalizing/ Mapping	- Prepare for highly textured and intersected narrative. - Separate understanding of the problematic from the people	- If people are not the problem and the problem is the problem, how would you name it? - As you think about the problematics that have been named how do they impact your day-to-day life and relationships with family, friends, and colleagues?
Story Sharing	- Allow participants to consider the problematic through mirrors and windows. - Consider personal impacts from an externalized and objective view.	- How does the problematic affect and effect you? - Beyond its immediate impacts, in what other areas of your life do you see the problematic, or response to it, impact you?

	- Notice how others are impacted and responding to the same stimuli.	- In the presence of _____ (any one or any combination of problematics), what does this invite you to do/not do, say/not say, think/not think?
Reverse Mapping	- Discover the presence of qualities and conditions (unique outcomes) that support alternative narratives.	- Are there times or experiences where the problematic was present but people acted in unexpected ways? Are there outcomes that seem to not be directed by the problematics listed? - What do you think is present that makes unique outcomes possible?
Naming a Preferred Narrative		- There are at least two well-defined narratives that people in this community/organization live into; if you had the opportunity to choose between them, do you have a preference?
Building a Transformative Strategy	- Build an action plan to advance the preferred narrative.	- What are the relationships, resources, and structures that would need to be transformed, so that it would become habit to live in the preferred narrative?

The next chapter will discuss skills necessary for successful facilitation. Some are basic facilitation skills. Others are unique to the narrative aspects of TCCs.

Chapter VII:
Skills for TCC
Facilitators

Transformative Community Conference facilitators do not require specialized training to facilitate a conference. Yet, there are certain facilitation practices that are helpful for a narrative-based process. A few of these practices are summarized in this chapter. For the facilitator that wants deeper theoretical and practical exposure to narrative facilitation, there are many other resources.[22]

Facilitated Engagement

The facilitator has primary responsibility for managing the content of a TCC. Usually facilitators have some experience with the community problematics.

A facilitator's actions are not "neutral." A facilitator influences the direction of storytelling. This presents a challenge: to make sure that the facilitator resists telling her or his own story, or allowing the conversation to focus on what's of interest or personal concern. A facilitator should increase clarity but also at times deconstruct or decompress a narrative to allow participants to identify additional openings for action or further conversation.[23] There are several strategies a facilitator can take to move a TCC forward.

Three facilitative strategies:
i. Deconstructive reflection
ii. Double Listening
iii. Naming the *absent but implicit* ideas

1. *Deconstructive Reflection*

The first style of facilitator intervention, ***deconstructive reflection***, involves using the participants' own words, as much as possible, to cause them to examine *the meaning* of their words. For instance, the following interaction took place during one of the Greensboro TCCs. During the practice round of the TCC, one participant was trying to name what they saw as the problematic being witnessed in the *third thing* (in this case, a play). The deconstruction, or breaking down, of commonly used terms allowed the speaker to be clear for themselves, allowed the audience (other participants) to appreciate all of the nuances of the speaker's words, and allowed the facilitator to avoid inserting her or his own interpretation in the community's narrative:

> **Speaker** *[in response to the facilitator's ongoing request to name the problematic]: Money, money.*
> **Facilitator:** *Money?*
> **Speaker:** *Everyone is operating [out] of a fear of not being paid, not having a job, wanting to make money, to have a hit to . . . It's major capitalism; commerce is a major problem.*

Facilitator: Okay, so when you started out, you talked about "money" and then the fear, but this is different. This isn't actually just fear; is there more specific fear or . . . ?

Speaker: Or yes, it's a . . . they work within a system. They work within a system where they have to behave a certain way to guarantee financial success.

Facilitator: Okay.

Speaker: Or financial survival; perhaps there are various levels of success.

Facilitator: All right, 'cause I'm trying to make sure I don't add my own meaning. So would you still say that the problem is best described as "money"? Would you label that money, and that would clear it up for you, or is there something else?

Speaker: There is a capitalist system. I might go with "capitalism" instead of money. Don't . . . look . . . I don't want to see those referenced as words of mine!

[Laughter by group].

Facilitator: All right.

In the exchange, "money" had multiple meanings. Each meaning—financial survival, currency, capitalism, commerce, and underpaying—would invite different stories, different narrative streams, for interpretation by other participants. Inviting the participant to name all of the meanings allowed others to connect to whichever they find to be the most resonant. At the same time, in this example, deconstructive reflection helped avoid the problem of the facilitator imposing her or his own chosen interpretation from among the available meanings.

Another example from the same phase of the Greensboro process shows how deconstructive listening can deepen and add texture to the mapping process. In this example, the participant is trying to characterize the problematic by referencing the actions of one of the play's main characters, Will Etta:

> *Participant: I wrote [in response to the prompt to name the problem] "personal experience versus conventional views."*
>
> *Facilitator: Personal experience versus conventional views?*
>
> *Participant: Yeah.*
>
> *Facilitator: Say more about that.*
>
> *Participant: Well, I think most of what Will Etta did and her version of authenticity versus how the director thinks she should be.*
>
> *Facilitator: Okay.*
>
> *Participant: And they are both trying to accommodate what would be in the best interest of the play, but the director is basing his direction off of a conventional view [of black women] versus Will Etta's actual experience of who she is.*
>
> *Facilitator: Okay, so distinguish that for me from the "misrepresentation" that was being spoken about earlier [by another participant that used "misrepresentation" as a description of the problematic].*
>
> *Participant: Oh, I think it's . . . I think there are, there is plenty of overlap, but . . .*
>
> *Facilitator: Okay.*

> *Participant: I guess what I'm saying about the misrepresentation . . . I see that my "conventional views" label is the cause of the misrepresentation.*
> *Facilitator: All right.*

The exchange allowed the facilitator to rely on the participant's actual words, while at the same time making it clear to the speaker and the other participants how language conveys different ideas. The exchange also allowed for a more nuanced mapping of problematics. By having the participant describe the relationship between his idea and an earlier one, the group could notice how conventional views were a source of misrepresentation. After this exchange, a facilitator would write on the easel board:

1. "Conventional views vs. personal experience" is labeled as a cause at the outer edge of the inner circle.
2. "Misrepresentation" is labeled as a spoke.

In this example, "conventional views vs. personal experience" still needs to be rooted in a core problematic. Later in the process when mapping the impacts, the facilitator could further explore with participants where the "views" versus "experience" distinction comes from (i.e., perhaps fear, isolation, or misinformation).

In summary, deconstructive listening is a facilitation strategy where a facilitator uses a participant's own words as a way to get them to explain what they mean by using those words, for the speaker's own benefit and for clarity for the other participants and the facilitator.

2. Double Listening

A second strategy, *double listening*, is an important tool for inviting participants to remain aware of both the problematics they are naming and also the resilient ways they have responded to the constraints of a dominant narrative. Michael White[24] reminds us that every person's life could be told by more than one story. Often when a person is telling a story that outlines a problematic narrative, the listeners do not hear other hopeful stories that could also be told, for example, how a person demonstrates resilience, creativity, and strength in response to constraints. By inviting another telling of a story, including some of the participant's response strategies to a problematic, the facilitator helps both the teller and the listeners realize they are not fully represented by a problem narrative.

> Every person's life could be told by more than one story.

The purpose is not to interrupt or minimize the impact of a problematic, but it is helpful from time to time to allow teller and listener to escape beyond the constraints of a problematic narrative. The other participants should know people by more than their stories of oppression or privilege. The facilitator, by inviting double listening, provides mirrors and windows—mirrors for the speaker to see themselves beyond the constraints of a particular story, and windows for others to look in and see more as well.

3. Naming Absent but Implicit Ideas

A third strategy for facilitators is to name what is *absent but implicit* in the ideas being discussed. This form is another aspect of double listening.

Jill Freedman summarizes Michael White on this point by saying:

> . . . a single description of any experience can be thought of as the visible side of a double description, and a story about a problem is made in contrast to some experience that is preferred and often treasured. If we listen closely, using what White has called "double listening," we can hear implications of the experiences that are being drawn on to make a distinction concerning the present experience. These *implied* experiences are a rich source of alternative stories . . . White called this sort of inquiry listening for the *absent but implicit*. White has listed, as examples, various meanings that we might understand to be implicit in people's discernments.[25]

The discernment of:	Is made possible by:
Frustration	- Specific purposes, values, and beliefs.
Despair	- Particular hopes, dreams, and vision for the future.
Injustice	- Specific conceptions of the just world.
Woundedness	- Specific notions of healing and wholeness.

Adapted from: White, M. (2003). Narrative practice and community assignments. International Journal of Narrative Therapy and Community Work. (2) pp. 17–55

Identifying what is absent but implicit is important because how we make sense of our circumstances is often by reference to the invisible and, therefore, unexamined. Unlike traditional forms of active listening and reflection, where a facilitator would either repeat back or paraphrase what has been said, **this practice requires identifying what is not said but is essential to make sense of what has been said.**

People live inside of stories that conform to broader narratives. In order to create future options, which currently do not seem possible, the narratives and stories have to be transformed. Often, in attempting community change, there will be an attempt to change only the narrative or stories. The absent but implicit ideas are invisible and mostly treated as "reality." In order to discover the most wide ranging transformation possible, not only the visible narratives must be addressed, but also those ideas that are usually invisible need to be made available for deconstructive reflection.

There are three steps involved in uncovering absent but implicit ideas:

1) to clarify for the speaker whether what is implied by what they say is what they want to imply;
2) to make implications visible to other participants, both for insight and to create the opportunity for either affirmation or deconstructive reflection;
3) when more than one idea can be implicit, it is helpful for the group to determine which (previously invisible) implication would be important for action planning; which implication makes room for greater transformation.

How a Facilitator Listens, Identifies, and Re-authors an Alternative Story

a) **Listen for positioning.** Inside the problem story, people are given and adopt positions as characters and plot elements. Somewhere in the way people are positioned shapes the trajectory of their language and performances. If these positions can be shifted, the plots and characterizations have the opportunity to change as well. When people tell a story about themselves or others, it is important to ask: "Who are you in this story?"

For example if a grandmother chooses, in response to the presence of fear, to not cooperate with a police officer who wants to speak to her grandchild, she might be positioned in the official narrative as being obstructive and somehow reinforcing poor behavior. Officers might actually characterize her as a *criminal accomplice*. If she is positioned as a criminal accomplice in the police version of the story, police are more likely to respond with less respect and to hear her through a filter of distrust. If the story is shifted, as opposed to the police officers being characterized as wanting to do harm, and the grandmother comes to understand that they see the child being influenced by elements that might not be healthy, the officers and grandmother might re-position each other as using the resources they have at their disposal to protect the child.

b) **Identify openings to an alternative story.** In looking for opportunities to transform a story we listen both for what is said (the problem story) and also what is not (double listening). The purpose is to uncover material to build an alternative, preferred narrative. For example, in the midst of a community debate over a new development project, many members of the community are frustrated because they sense that council members, who are the decision-makers, are misinformed. The constrained narrative held by council members describes the community members disparagingly as "protesters," while, in fact, the urgency expressed by community members actually reflects a deep commitment to making the decision-makers even more successful. By inquiring whether there has ever been a unique outcome where "protest," or testimony, gave the council members additional information that allowed them to make better decisions, the facilitator creates an opening for an alternative story about the community members' actions.

c) *Re-author the relationship story.* Based on the newly unveiled alternative story, the possibility exists to tell a new relationship story. The new relationship story is not affected in the same way by the constraining power of the previous story. For example, in the council–community members' community dispute mentioned above in (b), if the relationship is now characterized as decision-makers are "seeking advice and input from community members" as opposed to "protesting concerns," while the structure of interactions might be the same, the newly re-authored narrative supports improved listening.

Conclusion

Facilitating a Transformative Community Conference requires the skills of deconstructive reflection, double listening, and naming absent but implicit ideas. The purpose of using these skills is to listen for positioning, identify openings for an alternative story, and re-author relationship stories. Fundamentally, by employing their skills, facilitators will be able to transform problematics into preferred narratives. The next chapter explains what TCC facilitation looks like in action.

Chapter VIII:
Transformative
Community
Conferencing in Action

The Transformative Community Conferencing engagement model is new and evolving. The model grew out of efforts to apply restorative practices together with current understandings of the role of narratives in shaping and transforming people's lives. In this chapter there are three brief descriptions of early applications of the process: two community examples and one organizational example. The intention is to inspire the reader's imagination, not suggest that there are only certain ways to use the TCC model.

Racial Violence in Greensboro, NC

Greensboro was founded in 1808 as the county seat of Guilford County, North Carolina. Since founding, the town has existed as a crossroads community. A major railway junction for industrial and passenger rail, a highly industrial town with paper and textile mills, and a significant agricultural presence, Greensboro also sat at the edge of slavery and freedom. Although a town in the slaveholding southern United States, the first census in 1829 recorded 369 white residents, 101 slaves, and 26 free Blacks.[26] Greensboro boasts a progressive educational history. Colleges in town include Guilford College, which was founded by Quaker abolitionists as the first co-educational school in the state; Bennett College, an all-women's historically black college; Greensboro College, chartered by the Methodist Church as an all-women's (private) college; North Carolina A&T, a historically black state-funded school; and University of North Carolina–Greensboro, which was founded as an all-women's campus. Greensboro has also boasted a small but prominent Jewish community.

The presence of so many colleges and universities with progressive agendas made the community attractive for freedom seekers. Greensboro had both free and enslaved Blacks, which made it an important stop on the Underground Railroad. The Underground Railroad helped enslaved Africans in the south run toward the northern United States where slavery was not legal. Even during the Civil Rights movements of the 1950s and 1960s, the city was the site of important contributions to freedom and equity agendas. It was students from North Carolina A&T State University, Bennett College, and Guilford College, along with many middle class and working class Blacks, that conducted the first sit-ins at the downtown Woolworth's, seeking to racially integrate lunch counters and other public accommodations. Greensboro successfully introduced a mode of civil disobedience, which was studied and widely adopted across the country.

For all of its history of progressive activity, there is also a strong, organized conservative political presence in opposition. At times this included secessionist movements, the presence of the white supremacist Ku Klux Klan (KKK), and several efforts to resist unionization by the shuttering of various factories.

In addition to the events of November 1979, described below, there have been other recent events that have increased tensions, creating divisions in Greensboro. There have been accusations of police misconduct both from outside and inside the police force. Although Greensboro has been described as one of the most immigrant friendly cities in the south, there have been official actions (and some allegedly intentional inaction) that have left many in immigrant communities frightened and marginalized.

All of this is part of the backstory of Greensboro. The backstory continues to narrate the divisiveness of how the community relates to the events of November 1979, the subsequent trials, and the Greensboro Truth and Reconciliation Commission.

Traumagenic histories influence present day actions.

In November 1979, two groups, with what appear to be dramatically different views of the "best future" for Greensboro, were both holding demonstration marches in and around downtown Greensboro on the same day, at the same time. One group was composed of members of the KKK, the other composed mostly of people from the National

Association for the Advancement of Colored People (NAACP) and the Communist Workers' Party (CWP), who supported Black textile workers. The demonstration routes overlapped, resulting in a violent clash where several of the NAACP/CWP marchers, but none of the KKK, were injured or killed. There were criminal prosecutions of several members of the Klan who had participated in the march and were filmed during the march actively engaged in the violent acts. None were convicted of any crime. The outcomes of these trials reinforced the idea that there is a substantial difference in lived experiences among various segments of the Greensboro community.

In response to the clash, killings, and failure to convict, several activist groups, faith communities, and civil society organizations organized the Greensboro North Carolina Truth and Reconciliation Commission (GTRC). The GTRC implemented a process to address the racial violence in ways that supported an increased experience of unity for all residents.

An Excerpt from www.greensborotrc.org:

The Mandate of the Greensboro Truth and Reconciliation Commission (GTRC) reflects that, "There comes a time in the life of every community when it must look humbly and seriously into its past in order to provide the best possible foundation for moving into a future based on healing and hope."

[The GTRC] task was to examine the "context, causes, sequence and consequences," and to make

---

recommendations for community healing around the tragedy in Greensboro, N.C., on Nov. 3, 1979, which resulted in the deaths of five anti-Klan demonstrators: César Vicente Cauce, 25; Michael Ronald Nathan, M.D., 32; William Evan Sampson, 31; Sandra Neely Smith, 28; and James Michael Waller, M.D., 36.

The GTRC made important contributions toward a more just and equitable community and, yet, five years after the release of the official report, there were still perceived fractures in the community. To make progress on the goals of the GTRC, community members conducted an eighteen-month period of listening to assess the community's needs, aspirations, and values. During the listening process, one of the key observations was that there were many individuals and groups who were interested in—some already working toward—progress. The traditional relational patterns and some of the structural features of the community (i.e., transportation, perceived safety, location of available meeting spaces, and so on) resulted in groups working separately. The separation of efforts also produced differential access to information. As a result, groups came up with differing analyses of the problem and ultimately conflicting strategies for resolution.

There was an expressed desire, or at least willingness, among many of the separate groups to make connections to other similarly inclined groups and individuals. The TCC was presented and accepted as a model of engagement that could support an initial encounter.

Transformative Community Conferencing in Greensboro, NC

The Transformative Community Conference in Greensboro followed the steps outlined in the *Little Book*:

a. **Convening the right mix of people:** Identified approximately thirty-five to forty people who were active in different sectors—civil society, education, faith, advocacy, local government, business, and philanthropy—of the community, but who did not often work together.

b. **Conducted a practice dialogue, an analysis of a third thing:** Created an opportunity for all participants to view a play together. The intention of the play was to raise issues that are in some way representative of the issues facing the community. In this case, the play was a *Trouble in Mind* by Alice Childress, produced at the Triad Stage, a local theatre company. The following was a powerful exchange among some of the participants:

Male Speaker #7: For me it was a play about a misunderstanding, and therefore a misuse of power, that causes individuals to kind of nuance or be inauthentic as it relates to how we live, and therefore, just really complicating all the other relational connections that we have together as human beings. And then my takeaway was a more prophetic piece for me: who says that if we can do right and can really get into some kind of unity, that there is a divine commanded blessing associated with the struggle to get it right? And that was where the real hope that

I left with [was], because when I left [the theater], I was pretty frustrated and angry, because I still saw myself in some ways as living a life where I still have to nuance even if I detest it, but it's some fraction of my life I had to admit that I'm still nuancing my life. But the prophetic piece, the hope in it all for me, was that if you can keep attempting to move forward in some way to really find the kind of unity that can exist, that opportunity to find association or to command a blessing not just for me because I'm black or because you're white, but because we're human.

A TCC can be used to foster healing after racial violence.

Male Speaker #8: *What I take away from it is that people of color in particular are forced to contort themselves unnaturally to survive with racism, and more generally, that people are . . . there's some universal sense that people have to contort themselves to deal and survive with unchecked power, and the question that was raised to me is at what point do we . . . what is our breaking point? When just to be, [when just in order to] maintain our integrity, when do we say, "Enough?" And how far can we be pushed then before we have to just stop to say, "Enough?"*

Female Speaker #9: *I think also, I think for me it was about courage and lack of courage, different levels of courage, the courage to be who you are, to listen to someone else, to empathize. And the takeaway for me was futility, and sometimes not knowing who the man behind the screen is, because ultimately the guy that was*

99

making it hard for everyone is not really the guy that was controlling the action; that there is something behind the scenes and that sometimes when you're fighting, you don't remember who you're fighting, and maybe even why. You don't know who [or] where the "no" is actually coming from. And even if you have the courage to communicate, you're not always communicating with the person that has the most leverage or the solution.

The entire exchange was remarkable because participants were *externalizing the conversation,* describing problematics they personally struggle against, while linking it to the themes of the play. Participants identified several problematics in the first conversation—a dominant narrative, misinformation, economic constraints, and the use and misuse of power—that would show up again when *mapping community narratives.*

c. *Mapping community narratives*: After understanding the power of the narrative approach, participants conducted an analysis comparing the dominant with alternative narratives present in their community. The following is a partial summary of the narratives that were developed by community participants:

Facilitator: There is a story of Greensboro that is about mistrust, fear, how civility and a culture of politeness, duplicitousness, the drive of economics result in disempowerment, apathy, insularity, the protection of an image where people are punished for confronting the lie. They grow weary. They are invisible. They are silenced. There is a lack of a good vocabulary. There's apathy, segregation, an unwillingness to be vulnerable. There is

100

poor communications, and people . . . even those in the liberal class . . . operate in silos. That is a story that is available about Greensboro. We tell it all the time and you live into it and perform it every day when you get up and you walk outside.

And there's also a story in Greensboro where people take time. They persevere. They create a space for grace, forgiveness, and vulnerability. There's a leadership that allows for the creation of safe spaces, where trust can be built with cross-boundary interactions. There's a way in which people don't operate out of their history, where they've created opportunities for shared work and responsibility, bridging across communities, confronting economic barriers with people from many different communities who care more about friendship than they do about politics. There are many people who have not forgotten the ethic of love, and they've been able to build alliances across a wide spectrum to make common good. That story also exists in Greensboro.

Do you all have a preference? [Group laughter]

a. **Determining participants' preferred narrative:** It was essential to invite choice. Acknowledging the presence of multiple narratives, then stating a preferred narrative to live into, were the first acts of agency in support of transformation. This was not rushed. Participants in the Greensboro TCC needed to be given an opportunity to fully embrace and begin to embody the impact of choosing. In making a choice to support a different narrative, there would be habitual actions that they would need to give up.

101

b. **Building a transformation strategy:** During the reverse mapping of unique outcomes, participants were asked: "What are the qualities and conditions present (or absent) that make unique outcomes possible?" An action plan, a transformation strategy was created.

In Greensboro, among the problematics first addressed was the sense of full inclusion (separation) and safety for all residents (real and perceived fear). Out of the TCC process The Greensboro CounterStories Project was formed. The group's first effort was to respond to the presence of fear, marginalization, and exclusion and its many results and symptoms. The first project involved community members, police, and local government partners in a citywide discussion on the subject:

"How can we—as community, police, and local government—work together to build a Greensboro in which every resident and visitor feels included, protected, and respected?"

Their transformative strategy continues, guided by three TCC principles:

1. We have a preferred narrative;
2. Living into that preferred narrative is a daily choice
3. People aren't the problem, the problem is the problem!

Community Seeking Transformation: Newtown, Gainesville, GA

In April 1936, a tornado devastated several areas in the city of Gainesville, Georgia. One historical narrative of the city/county response to the devastation is that the political leadership seized the opportunity to relocate African Americans away from the central parts of the city. Beginning in 1937, the city developed a new part of town, Newtown, for its African American residents; many of the new houses in Newtown were built atop the disposal site of the storm debris. In the late 1940's and early 1950's, as a result of either intentional or lax zoning regulations, many highly polluting industries located in close proximity to the Newtown community. Over the next several decades a high number of deaths from cancer and other immune and autoimmune diseases raised concerns among a group of Newtown residents who formed an advocacy group called The Newtown Florists' Club. The club was so named because of the flowers they were buying for the high number of funerals and hospital visits that they associated with increased industrial pollution.

Although there were other predominantly African-American communities in close proximity to the concentration of industrial concerns, these communities had been historically inactive in terms of environmental advocacy.[27] Some leaders in Newtown suspected that the day-to-day struggles of economic concerns of maintaining personal employment or

A TCC can be used to foster healing after racial segregation.

responding to unemployment of family members caused these others to be less vocal. Gainesville was also the home of many poultry plants and textile mills that had attracted large numbers of Latino immigrants as factory workers to the community. The communities where the vast majority of Latino residents lived were also impacted by heavy concentrations of industrial pollutants, and yet these communities were seemingly absent from environmental advocacy forums.

Because Newtown is a small segment of the city of Gainesville, occupying only ten city blocks and composed of several dozen mostly elderly, poor, and working-class families, they lacked the political influence to force changes. But because of continuing advocacy, the group was able to garner some media and other attention.

The Newton Florists' Club was able to arrange a visit to the community from the Region IV Administrator of the Environmental Protection Agency (EPA). The visit was fairly high profile, attracting people from Newtown, other impacted communities, other people who had different environmental concerns, and businesses that were cautious of the potential impacts of increased EPA involvement. The regional administrator, Gwen Keyes Flemming, capitalized on this gathering to initiate a follow-up convening. The follow-up meeting took the form of an educational workshop where representatives of various community sectors—advocates, local and national businesses, civil society groups, faith communities, and local government—learned about EPA environmental standards and methods to file complaints or get EPA assistance in response to violations. At the conclusion of the workshop, EPA representatives informed the assembled community representatives that there were no environmental violations, in terms of clean air and water, and that the EPA did not have regulatory authority over noise, or some of the business interests of greatest concern such as junk yards, recycling plants, and rail transfer stations.

The outcome was not satisfying for many of the residents. They determined that even if no outside force could compel certain behaviors, the businesses would continue to make each others' lives less satisfying, unless they were able to establish a shared analysis of the problem and shared action plan to move forward. The community committed to a Transformative Community Conference. It was hoped that the TCC process would be a mechanism for them to build a shared vision for the future.[28]

Transformative Community Conferencing in Gainesville, GA.

A brief TCC process was conducted. While the Greensboro process occurred over the course of three months, the Gainesville process was one day. During the one-day TCC there was an opportunity to view a third thing video: A thirty-minute video that described an environmental collaborative from another state. The environmental issues in the video were substantially similar and also sufficiently distinct to serve as a third thing. They were similar in the sense that the pollution was clearly caused by the actions of various industrial operations. The important distinction, however, was that the industries in the film had been cited by regulators and admitted some level of responsibility. In fact, the industries had ceased operations. In that example the business, local government, federal government, and local community interests were aligned. In Newtown, the local industry had made efforts to improve, so they were no longer in violation of federal EPA standards, even though the community was still experiencing the negative impact of their operations. In Newton, the business, local government, and community interests were not aligned. The local government was also very protective of industry.

Participants at the TCC-styled workshop included Newtown activists, business representatives, leadership from other African American and Latino communities, and Gainesville residents who had an interest in extending parks, trails, and green spaces through Newtown and other nearby communities. The representatives were able to conduct an effective *mapping* and *reverse mapping* of the context presented in the video.

> A TCC can be used to foster healing after environmental degradation.

They were also able to broadly name the core problematics of their own community. However, because the communities were isolated and segregated from one another, there was not a shared sense of appreciation for the problematic descriptions coming from other communities. The limited amount of time did not allow for story sharing to deepen the sense of community and broaden the audience. In spite of the limitations, they were still able to effectively name an

106

alternative community narrative. Unique outcomes were identified but initially created conflict. The unique outcomes named by one sector of the community created resentments in other communities. For instance, where one community could point to the clean up of lots and the development of greenways, the other community could only express frustration having asked for and not received similar treatment.

By re-focusing on the assertion that "people are not the problem, the problem is the problem," the participants became united in their commitment to have equal government responses in all segments of the community. Certain issues that were previously only described as "problems for local community clean up" could now be connected to issues that impacted a larger segment of the community.

For example, the trails and greenways that might one day pass through or nearby Newtown became a concern for a broader spectrum of Gainesville residents. Community members focused on building trails could now see the impact of industrial activity in Newtown as connected to their desire for trail systems. The corresponding community plan was not simply an "environmental justice" plan. It became a preferred narrative. Environmental responsiveness became integrated with economic development and community beautification agendas. The new, alternative narrative also created buy-in from the educational community and the youth sports and recreation advocates who saw that it advanced their causes as well.

The Transformative Community conference in Gainesville determined a preferred narrative, establishing a shared future for many previously unaligned interests, allowing a collaborative transformative strategy benefiting all the parties.

Some Adaptions of TCC Methods for Working with Organizations

Transformative community conferences for organizations have a different starting point than conferences for community. Most organizations, especially not-for-profit, civil society, and philanthropic organizations, have a preferred narrative embedded in their organizational values. Values are usually reflected in vision and mission statements. What often happens that makes a Transformative Community Conference desirable in an organization is that the internal (and sometimes the external) operational practices do not align with the employees and clients' expectations for the way the organizational values should be performed. It is sometimes the case that values have become embedded in a historical way of operating that is either invisible and needs to be unveiled or the way of performing a value has become outdated and needs to be updated to reflect new employees and clients.

In these cases, transformative conference processes can be used to achieve *narrative alignment*.

Narrative alignment occurs when the relationship patterns, resource allocations, and organizational structures reflect the organizations central values.

On some rare occasions, the values have to be restated or completely discarded to reflect the organization's current commitments. More often, what is required is re-alignment. As a result the organizational process has most of the same elements as other TCC processes, with some necessary adaptations:

a. **Third thing/practice mapping**: A valuable approach to a third thing for an organization is a movie, video, or documentary, preferably an inspirational one that reminds the members of the organization of *why* they are doing the work that they do in the first place.

b. **Problematic mapping**: For an organization it is important to highlight the central organizational values as a first step in the mapping process. The conferencing process should not seek to remake the organization, but rather to re-orient the operations in alignment with the agreed upon value commitments. If the organizational values are clear and present, the naming of the problematic comes in reference to the failure to adequately represent these values. For example:

Facilitator: We start from the premise that people are not the problem. The problem is the problem. Given that your central organizational values are for [i.e., full inclusion, respect for diversity, creativity, asset-focused leadership, and future thinking], how would you name the problematics that you are experiencing?

The purpose is to keep the analytical focus inside the container of the current organizational structure. However, the facilitator should be aware that if the problems are significant, the participants might push against the current structures and invite deeper structural reconsiderations. Either way, the standard conferencing process will continue with mapping and reverse mapping.

c. *Importance of creating time for story sharing:* Organizations are even more closely woven and impacted by the stories that are told than are communities. Because the organizational community is typically made up of fewer people, single voices or small numbers can have disproportionate impacts. Each individual story has the capacity to touch a higher portion of people than in an entire community; additionally, stories reverberate in the sense that they are repeated often in the small container of the organization. This is not an encouragement to allow single voices of dissent to drive the direction of the organization. However, there is significant value in creating spaces where stories can be told and the teller can receive some affirmation. It is especially important here for the facilitator to name absent but implicit meanings, so they can be explored, and so a single, dominant story can be situated in the context of other stories.

Conclusion

Racial violence, racial segregation, and environmental degradation are all significant issues with deep-seated impacts. Transformative Community Conferencing offers a hopeful, practical approach to dialogue, building transformative strategies for meaningful change. The communities in Greensboro and Gainesville currently operating out of preferred narratives are examples that real change is possible.

So, now what? How can you get started with TCCs? We turn to these questions now in the final chapter.

Chapter IX:
Now What?—
Conclusion

Transformative Community Conferencing is a new model of community engagement and dialogue that:

1. Makes dominant community and organizational problematics and narratives more visible.
2. Conducts an analysis of the relations of power that sustain and reproduce dominant narratives.

Thus, TCCs expose structures of community and organizational life that result in experiences of marginalization, oppression, and/or exclusion.

3. Identifies several examples of unique outcomes, actions, and other indicators that point to alternative, preferred narratives.
4. Presents participants with the opportunity to collaboratively narrate and collectively state a preference among competing narratives.

5. Provides a foundation from which to build a transformative action plan that supports the reshaping of relationships, reallocation of resources, and redesign of systems and structures in ways that align with preferred narratives.

Thus, TCCs create integrated, equitable, and/or inclusive communities and organizations.

TCCs are implemented based on an understanding that all people live inside of narratives. Narratives are powerful, influencing a person's thoughts, feelings, and behaviors. Relationships with others are performed by how each person is positioned within narratives. In the same way, the structures that exist in a community or organization make sense inside of dominant narratives. Where disparities and inequities persist, systems consciously and unconsciously serve to sustain and reproduce dominant narratives.

Narrative Theory

Transformative Community Conferencing is based on narrative theory, but it is sufficiently simple to implement. The convener, facilitator, and participants do not need to understand narrative theory in order for the process to be successfully implemented.

TCCs are also hope-filled practices. The foundational action of TCC practice does not blame or demonize any particular person or group. The foundational assertion—the people aren't the problem, the problem is the problem—creates a welcoming and invitational space for all members of a community or organization, regardless of whether they are helped, harmed, completely unaffected, or even unaware of the constraints created by the dominating narratives. Oppression, marginalization, violence, disparity, and exclusion are not inevitable features of community. Disengagement, voicelessness, and despair associated with misaligned priorities are not inevitable features of organizational life. **The hopefulness of the TCC asserts that when people have the opportunity to examine the narratives that guide and organize their day-to-day lived experiences, they will choose to transform their lives by actively transforming the narratives they act into.**

The rhythm and spiral nature of TCC implementation gives participants the opportunity to look into metaphorical mirrors, of their own experience, and look through metaphorical windows, to understand and develop an appreciation for the experiences of others. Externalizing the problematics that shape their lives and mapping the impacts to multiple levels allows for a nonjudgmental, yet deeply engaged, collaborative analysis. Identifying unique outcomes provides the basis for the collective statement of a preferred narrative and direction.

TCCs have shared features and important distinctions with other conflict-resolution, problem-solving, justice-seeking, and reconciliation processes. The

115

application of a TCC is not intended to replace other processes. Rather, the TCC can be the first analysis and planning process that allows a community or organization to understand how, when, and why to apply other approaches.

Transformation is a long-term agenda. When the dominant narrative has produced and reproduced a history of division and brokenness, reconciliation becomes one goal of transformation efforts.

Reconciliation

Reconciliation is a complex and interwoven set of processes that have as a shared aim the production and affirmation of identities that are Relationally constructed, Authentic, Dignified, Interconnected, and Legitimated, emphasizing performatively co-equal (radically co-equal) communities and organizations.

TCCs produce a foundational analysis that allows the community or organizational members to determine which relationships, resources, and structures must be strengthened, transformed, or eliminated in support of the preferred narratives and radically co-equal identities.

As a new model of engagement, there are likely to be many variations and applications of the process. **That's where you come in . . .**

Notes

1. White, M., & Epston, D. (1990). Narrative Means to Therapeutic Ends. *New York, NY: WW Norton.*

2. Winslade, J., & Monk, G. (2001). Narrative Mediation: A New Approach to Conflict Resolution. San Francisco, CA: Jossey-Bass.

3. Winslade, J., & Monk, G. (2001). *Narrative Mediation: A New Approach to Conflict Resolution.* San Francisco, CA: Jossey-Bass.

4. White, M., & Epston, D. (1990). *Narrative Means to Therapeutic Ends.* New York, NY: WW Norton.

5. Austin, J. L. (1962). *How to Do Things with Words* (2nd ed.). (J. O. Urmson, & M. Sbisa', Eds.) Cambridge, MA: Harvard University Press.

6. Lederach, J. P., & Lederach, A. J. (2010). *When Blood and Bones Cry Out.* New York: Oxford University.

7. Zehr (2002). *The Little Book of Restorative Justice.* Intercourse, PA: Good Books Publications p 19.

8. Mamdani, M. (2012). *Define and Rule: Native as Political Identity.* Cambridge, MA: Harvard University Press.

9. Foucault, M. (1994). *Power.* (J. D. Faubion, Ed., & R. Hurley, Trans.) New York, New York: The New Press.

10. Lederach, J. P., & Lederach, A. J. (2010). *When Blood and Bones Cry Out.* New York: Oxford University.

11. Rock, D. (2009). *Your Brain at Work: Strategies for Overcoming Distraction, Regaining Focus, and Working Smarter All Day Long.* New York, NY: HarperCollins.

12. Cobb, S. (2013). *Speaking of Violence.* New York, NY: Oxford University Press.

13. Nelson, H. L. (2001). *Damaged Identities Narrative Repair.* Ithica, NY: Cornell University Press.

14. Monk, G. and Winslade J. (2013). *When Stories Clash: Addressing Conflict With Narrative Mediation.* Taos, NM: Taos Institute Publications

15. Denborough, D. (2008). *Collective Narrative Practice: Responding to individuals, groups, and communities who have experienced trauma.* Adelaide, South Australia: Dulwich Center Publications

16. Palmer, P. (2004). *A Hidden Wholeness: The Journey Toward an Undivided Life.* San Francisco, CA: Jossey-Bass.

17. Freire, P. (1970). *Pedagogy of the Oppressed.* New York: Continuum Books.

18. Cobb, S. (2013). *Speaking of Violence.* New York, NY: Oxford University Press.

19. VeneKlassen, L. W. (2002). *A New Weave of Power, People, and Politics.* (D. Budlender, & C. Clark, Eds.) Warwickshire, UK: Practical Action Publishing.

20. Foucault, M. (1980). *Power/Knowledge.* New York: Pantheon Books.

21. Monk, G., Winslade, J., Crocket, K., & Epston, D. (Eds.). (1997). *Narrative Therapy in Practice: The Archeology of Hope.* San Franciisco, CA: Jossey-Bass. p. 108

22. Denborough, D. (2010). Narrative practice as conflict dissolution/social-historical healing. In D. Denborough, *Socio/Historical Conflict Dissolution.* Adelaide: Dulwich Centre; McCarthy, J. (2004).

Enacting Participatory Development: Theatre-Based Technices. Lundon, UK: Earthscan.; Monk, G., & Winslade, J. (2013). *When Stories Clash.* Taos, New Mexico: Taos Institute Publications; Winslade, J., & Monk, G. (2001). *Narrative Mediation: A New Approach to Conflict Resolution.* SanFrancisco, CA: Jossey-Bass.

23. Cobb, S. (2013). *Speaking of Violence: The Politics and Poetics of Narrative in Conflict Resolution (Explorations in Narrative Psychology).* New York: Oxford.

24. White, M. (2007). *Maps of Narrative Practice.* New York, NY: WW Norton & Co.

25. http://www.familycentre.org.nz/Publications/PDF's/ Freedman_Absent_but_Implicit.pdf. Evanston Family Therapy Center Website Accessed April 5, 2016

26. http://www.greensboro-nc.gov/index.aspx?page = 142

27. Johnson-Gaither, C. (2014). 'Smokestacks, Parkland, and Community Composition: Examining Environmental Burdens and Benefits in Hall County, Georgia, USA.' *Environment and Behavior,* 1020.

28. Mueller, S. (2012, Dec 28). *Gainesvilletimes.com.* Retrieved Nov 7, 2015, from Hall County Hamlets: http://www.gainesvilletimes.com/flat/hamlets/.

About the Author

D*avid Anderson Hooker* is an Associate Professor of the Practice of Conflict Transformation at the Kroc Institute for International Peacebuilding in the Keough School of Global Affairs at University of Notre Dame. He has been a mediator, facilitator, and community builder since 1982. In his practice, he has assisted groups, organizations, congregations, communities, and local and national governments in conducting important conversations on difficult subjects. He was the Research and Training Director for Coming to the TABLE (Taking America Beyond the Legacy of Enslavement) and a co-designer of the Greensboro Counter Stories Project. The ideas in this *Little Book* were also formulated through his work in post conflict communities in Bosnia, Cuba, Myanmar, Nigeria, Somalia, and South Sudan as well as many communities throughout the United States.